Delighting in Jesus

A Key to Effective Spiritual Leadership

Gil Stieglitz

Delighting in Jesus: A Key to Effective Spiritual Leadership

©2015 Gil Stieglitz
Published by Principles to Live By, Roseville CA 95661
www.ptlb.com

Cover by John Chase
Copyedited by Jennifer Edwards and Sandy Johnson

All rights reserved. No part of this publication may be reproduced, stored in a retrieval system, or transmitted in any way by any means—electronic, mechanical, photocopy, recording, or otherwise—without the prior permission of the copyright holder, except as provided by USA copyright law.

All Scripture verses are from the New American Standard Bible unless otherwise indicated. New American Standard Bible: 1995 update. 1995 La Habra, CA: The Lockman Foundation.

Due to the sensitive subject matter, names and other identifying information have been altered to protect the privacy of those whose stories and quotes are included in the book.

ISBN 978-0-9909641-3-1
Christian Living

Printed in the United States of America

Dedication

This book is dedicated to the Lord Jesus Christ.
May His name and His glory be exalted.
May those that read this book and do its exercises
find new levels of delight in the Savior of the World.

Table of Contents

Introduction..7

Chapter 1: The Baptism of Jesus................................19

Chapter 2: The Temptation of Christ..........................35

Chapter 3: Jesus Visits His Hometown........................57

Chapter 4: The Feeding of the Five Thousand.................85

Chapter 5: Jesus Walks on the Water...........................109

Chapter 6: The Parable of the Sower...........................135

Chapter 7: The Problem of Tragedy............................157

Chapter 8: Jesus Teaches on Prayer - Part 1.................173

Chapter 9: Jesus Teaches on Prayer - Part 2.................197

Chapter 10: The Widow's Mites..................................215

Conclusion..227

Bibliography...231

About the Author..233

Delighting in Jesus
Introduction

This brief look at a few of the scenes in Jesus' life will orient the thinking person to many of the nuances of His teaching. While the episodes in this portfolio are random, they are significant in exploring the life and ministry of Jesus. Each one of these lessons explores one scene in the life of Jesus and, it will allow you to take delight in Jesus in a different way. The wonder in the gospel accounts of Jesus is in exploring the unique life of Jesus the Son of God and being surprised and changed by what He said. Spend time with Jesus in the warp and woof of His life and you will become more delighted in Him. These notes are not meant to be exhaustive accounts of these parts of Jesus' life, but they are designed to bring a new perspective to Jesus.

The Apostle John says at the end of his book about Jesus, *"And there are also many other things which Jesus did, which if they were written in detail, I suppose that even the world itself would not contain the books that would be written."* Therefore it is impossible for me to tell you all of the ways to delight in Jesus. I want to just provide you a few ways to probe into the wonder of Jesus and find yourself delighted with Him. He is fully human and fully divine. He can empathize with our infirmities and can now understand the depths of God. He is for us and wants our lives to follow His plan for us as that is what will suit us best.

I have found that a number of Christians, while believing in Jesus as their Savior, do not know enough about Him or delight in Him nearly enough. He is amazing and deserves our full attention. In the pages that follow I have included various glimpses of the wonder of Jesus the Christ. Each of these chapters will look at a different episode in Jesus' earthly life or an overall picture of His wonder. Take delight in Him for He is God. In each chapter or at the conclusion of each chapter I have included an exercise to heighten your delight in Jesus.

Let me start off immediately with an exercise in delighting in Jesus.

Titles and Ministries of Jesus
The following are the titles and ministries of Jesus Christ in our lives. He is, at this very moment, attempting to be these wonderful things in your life. Pray slowly through these actions of our Lord and press into where Jesus is trying to minister to you. Agree to cooperate with Him in these ministries. Let Him speak to you about how He is moving in your life and how He is trying to be your God in these ways if you would allow Him.

1. What three ministries of Jesus has He been to you in the last three months?

2. Circle the ways you can see Jesus being active in your life as you reflect back on the last three months.

Introduction

"I AM" (John 8:58)
From the Hebrew Old Testament verb "to be" signifying a living, intelligent, and personal being, "I AM" means that Jesus is the living God who is outside time and pulsating with life. He is powerfully active in that moment in your life.

SOTER - "Savior" (Luke 1:47)
Jesus is the Savior of all mankind. He is the only way to achieve forgiveness, righteousness, and grace in order to be able to approach God. As our savior this means that Jesus is offering Himself to forgive you and energize you to live a life above what is capable for you so that you can connect directly with the Almighty God.

JESUS (Luke 1:31)
From the Hebrew "Joshua" meaning JEHOVAH (Yahweh) IS SALVATION. The name means that Jesus is God and is offering Himself as the way to avoid God's wrath because of our sin and rebellion, while at the same time delivering us into God's presence and into a right relationship with Him.

CHRIST
This is equivalent to the Hebrew "Messiah" (Meshiach), "The Anointed One." This means that Jesus is the long-awaited Messiah (Special Leader) of the Jewish people who opened a way to God for the Jews and Gentiles. This means that Jesus is your anointed leader and savior. Have you allowed Him to lead you, or are you still trying to make all the decisions?

SHEPHERD OF THE SHEEP (Hebrews 13:20)
Jesus is looking out for His flock. As our shepherd He cares, directs, lifts up, makes rest, feeds, corrects, and comforts those who believe in Him. He leads His sheep to green pastures and beside quiet streams. He makes them lie down from the frenetic pace they would keep without Him. He corrects them and tips them back up when they have fallen and cannot get back up. He will, at times, break the leg of a rebellious and overly curious sheep and carry it on His shoulders so that it learns to stay close to Him. He is setting up a banquet in full view of your enemies so that His love can be displayed to you and to them. Are you letting this happen?

MASTER (2 Timothy 2:21)
By virtue of His person and work in creation and salvation, Jesus is the Master of all -- especially of believers. This means that Jesus will come to us as our master and direct us to do something for Him. There will be times when He tells you, "No, I do not want you to go that way," or "This other way is my way for you." He is the Master and He knows more than we do. Are you resisting what is clearly His will for you?

KING OF KINGS (1 Timothy 6:15; Revelation 17:14)
Jesus is the King that is above all kings and political rulers. This means that Jesus will at times force political rulers to acknowledge that they must follow His laws and live by His code of conduct. It is easy to be caught up in the political events of our day instead of realizing that we serve the ultimate King above all political rulers. Take a step back and let Jesus lead you on your mission that is a part of His grander plan.

Introduction

LORD OF LORDS (Revelation 19:11-16)
Jesus is the leader above all leaders. This means that He will assert His position of supreme leader over all other leaders -- vocational, governmental, familial, and personal. Even though other leaders may try and impose their standards upon us, Jesus is still the one we follow. He will have us follow Him even though the world will tell us that some new standard is the way to live. He is the ultimate Lord, so follow His rules. Is He trying to get your attention before you adopt a worldly standard instead of a godly standard?

BISHOP AND GUARDIAN OF OUR SOULS
(1 Peter 2:25)
Jesus is the one who oversees our life, pointing out what direction to go and which areas to avoid. This means that Jesus is actively leading and warning us about what is happening in our life. Jesus is specifically trying to help you live a better life. He is overseeing it and trying to guard your soul. Are you fighting His work of supervision in your life? Are you allowing Him to steer you away from the wrong friends or destructive activities? Are you letting Him fulfill His ministry of guarding your soul?

DELIVERER (Romans 11:26)
Jesus is our deliverer from the wrath of God but also our deliverer from current spiritual, mental, emotional, and physical danger. He is active in His deliverance of us if we will follow His lead. Jesus told us that He would always send a way of escape when we are in over our heads. We just have to take it when it comes. We cling to Jesus as our deliverer

from our sins, and we look to His specific practical deliverances throughout our life.

ADVOCATE (1 John 2:1, 2; Hebrews 7:25)
An advocate is a defense attorney that keeps us from being punished and jailed. This means that Jesus pleads for our release from the eventual penalty of our sins; but also He pleads against the current accusations of the Devil, the world, and our own mind. He defends us before the justice of God, others, and ourselves. Are you adding to the list of things that He needs to defend you before the Father? Celebrate His work on your behalf but celebrate when you avoid sin.

SECOND ADAM (Romans 5:12, 14, 15)
The first Adam failed to be God's perfect representative, but Jesus as the second Adam lived the perfect life and voluntarily gave up His life so that His righteousness could spread to all who believe. This means that Jesus right now is seeking to spread His righteousness through your obedience and actions. When you know how Jesus lived in complete dependence upon the Holy Spirit and the Father, then you can follow His example. He listened and obeyed. What is God whispering in your spirit about your life?

CHIEF CORNERSTONE (Ephesians 2:20-23)
Jesus is the first and crucial part of the foundation of a whole new way of approaching God. God wanted people to approach Him in an accurate and appropriate way and that way is through Jesus Christ. He is constructing a new Temple

to God out of those who believe in Him as the Son of God and their Savior. Jesus wants to fashion us into a wonderful instrument of worship so that you, being who you were made to be, will vibrate with a beautiful melody to God. Is your life in harmony with what Jesus is and what he wants you to be?

IMMANUEL (Matthew 1:23; Revelation 21:3-5)
Immanuel means God with us. Jesus is the full representation of God in human flesh living among us. If we want to know what God is like, then look at how Jesus acted. He was not just a prophet but God in flesh. When we are confused by God's actions in our life, we can go back to the gospels and find God explained in human form in Jesus. Our erroneous ideas about God diminish our trust in Him. But when we look at the life of Jesus, we see God and we find the answers that we need.

FIRST BORN (Revelation 1:5)
Jesus bears the special title of the first born which connotes the supreme position. It means that He is leader and ruler over everything that follows. As God began the creation of our universe, He allowed Christ -- the second person of the Tri-unity -- to do all the creating. He did this so that Christ would be in supreme position over everything in this universe. Have you placed Him in the supreme position in your life over every area and decision?

HEAD OF THE BODY (Colossians 1:18)

Jesus is the director, leader, and coordination point of all the actions of the true Christian Church. He is the head of all the individual churches and the head over all the churches collectively. When the church listens to His direction, it is no longer spasmodic and unproductive. Where do you fit within His church? It is not possible to be directed by Jesus and not be helping some part or aspect of His church. What is your part?

ROOT OF JESSE (Romans 15:12)

Jesus is the descendant of David, the great King of Israel, whose father was Jesse. Jesus is the fulfillment of the promise made to David centuries before that His Son would rule over the people of Israel forever. Jesus unites Jew and Gentile believers as one who comes from the root of Jesse. Are you a unite-er? Are you embracing your role as a link between generations of believers? Is God asking you to reach back to an early generation and embrace your common faith with those who may appear different but who really are brothers or sisters in faith?

STONE (Romans 9:33; Ephesians 2:20)

Jesus is the stone that those who are trying to work their way to heaven stumble over on their way to God. It is not possible to be perfect from our human starting place. God the Father has made Him the Chief Cornerstone for a whole new way of approaching God -- the way of faith. Righteousness is obtained before God through faith, not works. When you try and please God in your own power and effort, the stone comes and crushes all you have built. But when you admit that your works don't connect you to God, Jesus Christ, the stone, allows you to build a life on Him as a foundation. What are you doing? Building your own life trying to please yourself or God or building on the rock, which is Jesus?

CHIEF APOSTLE (Hebrews 3:1)
All the apostles were sent by Jesus to tell the good news that there was a way opened to God that did not require perfection -- it only required faith in the one sent from God. Jesus was the One sent from the Father to us with the message of salvation – He is that message. As Jesus is trying to be the chief apostle in your life, He could be asserting His ability to make the rules you live by, or he could be seeking to send you as one of His sent ones to a lost and dying world that is all around you. Which is it?

GREAT HIGH PRIEST (Hebrews 4:14)
The great high priest of Israel made sacrifices for sins once a year; and in order to cover the sins of the people, he poured the blood of a spotless lamb on the mercy seat that resided in the Holy of Holies. Jesus is our great High Priest, who was the perfect sacrifice and entered into the Heavenly Holy of Holies to pour His own blood out before the Father as the perfect sacrifice for our sins. When you sin, it is Jesus who approaches the Father and makes atonement for your sin. Feel the power of His ministry on your behalf.

PIONEER AND PERFECTER OF OUR FAITH, OR AUTHOR AND FINISHER (Hebrews 12:2)

Jesus was the first of the way of faith and was Himself the way. On the cross He kept entrusting Himself to the One who judges righteously and that what God had asked Him to do was right, just, good, and propitiatory. His faith was rewarded with the offer of righteousness to all who would believe in Him, and He was given a name that is above all other names. He saw your faith down through the corridors of time and was hopeful that you would nurture your faith as you saw Him trusting and perseverant in paying for your sins. Jesus pioneered the type of faith He is looking forward to seeing in you. Trust Jesus and move forward.

LAMB OF GOD (John 1:29)

In order to cleanse the sins of the people of Israel, a spotless lamb had to be sacrificed in the people's place. John the Baptist cried out that Jesus was the spotless Lamb of God who would be sacrificed for the sins of the whole world. Jesus willingly gave up His perfect life so we could have life. Meditate upon His sacrifice so you could be healed from the infection of sin.

LORD GOD ALMIGHTY (Revelation 21:22)

Jesus is called the Lord God Almighty and functions in that role of Supreme Ruler of the Universe. Jesus is called the Lord God Almighty and will one day reveal to the whole world this role that He now holds. We live in this unique place in history where God wants His believers to display that He is the Lord God Almighty in and through their lives so that more will repent and embrace Jesus Christ. How is your display of Christ as Lord God Almighty going?

LOGOS (John 1:1-5, 14; Hebrews 1:1-3; Rev. 19:11-13)
John the Apostle uses the term Logos to describe Jesus in eternity. He was and is the eternal Word. Jesus is the distinct person within the One God who is the eternal expression of the Triune God. Look again at the person of Jesus we see in the gospels and marvel at the real God wrapped in humanity.

SOPHIA (Colossians 2:2, 3)
Jesus is described as the summation of all of the treasures of wisdom and knowledge. Spend time looking at His wisdom in the Sermon on the Mount in Matthew 5-7 or the knowledge He displayed in the Olivet Discourse in Matthew 24, 25. He is wisdom defined. What wisdom do you need right now? How is Jesus trying to get you the wisdom you need? Are you ready to receive it?

ALPHA AND OMEGA (Revelations 1:8; 21:6; 22:13)
This is the beginning and ending letters of the Greek alphabet. Jesus takes this title because just as in writing, one uses the alphabet in order to communicate. To write anything one must use the alphabet. You never need to go outside of Jesus for faith and life -- He is all you need. We are tempted to think that we need the latest thing the world is offering or some expensive thing from the past, but Jesus is the beginning and the ending. We really just need Him. Are there things that you think you must have? Is Jesus trying to help you see

that you don't need them? One day the world will all sum up in Jesus. He will be the Omega. Find in Him and through Him what you need for life. Are there people that He is trying to insert into your life? Are there activities He is trying to have you try? Are there perspectives that He is trying to get you to consider? If you stay only with your own wisdom, your own relationships, or your own activities, you will miss out on what the Alpha and Omega has in mind for you. Don't miss out!

1. Go back over the list and put an X by the ones you need Jesus to be for you in the next three months.

2. Pray and ask Christ to show Himself strong in the ways you have just marked.

Chapter 1
The Baptism of Jesus

Key Verses

Matthew 3:13-17 - *Then Jesus arrived from Galilee at the Jordan coming to John, to be baptized by Him. But John tried to prevent Him, saying, "I have need to be baptized by You, and do You come to me?" But Jesus answering said to him, "Permit it at this time; for in this way it is fitting for us to fulfill all righteousness." Then he permitted Him. And after being baptized, Jesus went up immediately from the water; and behold, the heavens were opened, and he saw the Spirit of God descending as a dove, and coming upon Him, and behold, a voice out of the heavens, saying, "This is My beloved Son, in whom I am well-pleased."*

Mark 1:9-11 - *And it came about in those days that Jesus came from Nazareth in Galilee, and was baptized by John in the Jordan. And immediately coming up out of the water, He saw the heavens opening, and the Spirit like a dove descending upon Him; and a voice came out of the heavens: "Thou art My beloved Son, in Thee I am well-pleased."*

Luke 3:21-23 - *Now it came about when all the people were baptized, that Jesus also was baptized, and while He was praying, heaven was opened, and the Holy Spirit descended upon Him in bodily form like a dove, and a voice came out of heaven, "Thou art*

My beloved Son, in Thee I am well-pleased." And when He began His ministry, Jesus Himself was about thirty years of age, being supposedly the son of Joseph, the son of Eli...

The Story Detailed

Jesus' baptism marked the official beginning of His ministry. It was with this action that He announced the commencement of His mission to save the world. It seems like Jesus would immediately start ministering, but He didn't. He went through a formal process of presenting Himself first to God's representative (John the Baptist) to be baptized. It is very instructive to see how Jesus began His ministry. It has huge implications for us today, especially with our haphazard and cavalier orientation toward ministry.

1. John Baptized and Proclaimed the Coming Kingdom

John the Baptizer had been preaching and baptizing people for about three months as he made His way up the Jordan River, north toward the Sea of Galilee. His message was clear: "Make yourself ready, for the kingdom is coming." This event took place during a Sabbatical year the last week of December 26, A.D. or the first week of January 27, A.D. A Sabbatical year lasted from October to October and was a time when the people were released from business and other obligations. This probably accounted for the large crowds that John attracted.

John understood His prophetic role as the one who would "make straight the way of the Lord" (John 1:23). It was revealed to him that he would recognize the Messiah, the Son of God, by a special sign -- the Holy Spirit descending on a man in the form of a dove remaining there (John 1:32-34). He was waiting for the King to come. Imagine what John must have been feeling as he waited for the special person upon whom the Spirit would descend.

2. Jesus Responded to the Call

Since He was twelve years old Jesus had been waiting to be about His Father's business. He knew early on that He was the King of the kingdom but did not know *when* He was to move out of His private life and into His public ministry, and He also did not know *how* it would come about. Among the Jews there was a great anticipation that the Messiah must be about to appear since there were only three to four more years left on Daniel's prophecy timeline. (Daniel 9:25-26 describes a time when the Messiah would be cut off.) There was also great anticipation among the Jews about the Messiah being among them because the scepter had departed from Shiloh years before when the Romans had taken from them the right to capital punishment. The thinking was that the Messiah must be alive. He just hadn't been revealed yet.

At last the announcement Jesus had been waiting for started to circulate -- "Get ready, because the long-awaited kingdom is coming!" Through John the Baptist God had set His world-changing mission in motion. Imagine Jesus' thoughts as He walked the twenty miles to the place where He heard John was baptizing: "Is it time now? How will it happen?" He was about thirty years old at this point in His life. He had been waiting a long time.

Jesus' baptism didn't include repentance from His sins because He was sinless. Rather, it was a way to identify with the movement that longed for the kingdom of God. He wanted the kingdom of God to come as much as, if not more than, any person ever did. Some have suggested that He was carrying the sins of the world at that point and thus needed to be baptized, but this is unsound. God the Father laid the sins of the world on Christ while He was on the cross groaning, "My God, My God, why hast Thou forsaken Me?"

Jesus approached the place in the Jordan where John was baptizing the crowds, waiting until the end of the day after all the other people had been baptized (Luke 3:21). He did not draw attention to Himself, but He was patient and unhesitating. As John was about to finish, Jesus stepped forward. He was ready to begin -- it was time.

3. John Recognized His Unworthiness

John did not recognize Jesus right away (John 1:31, 33), and he did not fully understand who He was at first. Even though they were cousins, it is most likely that they had never met as adults though John must have heard the story from His mother about this special child six months His junior. All that John knew was that He would recognize the King, the Messiah, the Lamb of God once the dove came down and rested upon someone. Certainly John did not realize that the Messiah would be God in human flesh -- the One who created the world, the Alpha and the Omega, the Beginning and the End.

But John was sharp enough to realize there was something special about this man Jesus. The one who stepped out of the fleeing multitude was special. We are not told what tipped Him off but something did. There is something about Jesus that draws you to Him.

Immediately upon seeing Jesus, John recognized the juxtaposition between people and thus responded in genuine humility: "I need to be baptized by you," he said. John was right, but this was not about superiority. It was about getting started in the right way. John was the herald of the coming Kingdom and would baptize the Messiah.

Up to that point Jesus had baptized no one, but He would soon be baptizing people into the kingdom of God. Jesus declared that John's baptism was a heavenly baptism meant to prepare people for the coming kingdom through repentance of sins. God had allowed John to get lots of people ready, and it was now time for Jesus to start His public ministry of actually offering the kingdom of God. John was not a member of this new kingdom but was a key bridge to the new covenant in Jesus. Notice how Jesus talks about John later: "Yet the one who is least in the kingdom of heaven is greater than he [John the Baptist]" (Matthew 11:7-14).

4. Jesus Replied

Though John tried to prevent Jesus' baptism, Jesus responded graciously and kindly with an intelligent response to a theological impossibility: "Permit it at this time," He says. He explained to John that going through the process of baptism would fulfill all righteousness. The King needed to identify with the movement he was leading and demonstrated that He wanted the kingdom also. Technically Jesus didn't need to be baptized, but baptism was an important symbol and identification with the movement of Kingdom readiness. He was all in on wanting the Kingdom, especially as He was bringing it. It is interesting that Jesus was willing to obey little rules and symbolic gestures in order to speak to different types of people. He did not use His obvious authority as a way to get out of these rules and customs. It is significant when the king is willing to be subject to the laws He enacts. We see another instance of this with the poll tax episode later in His ministry. He proved to Peter that he did not need to pay the tax, but He paid it anyway in a miraculous way. There was none of the "I am the King" attitude.

This baptism seemed like a small thing, but it helped fulfill all righteousness. It was one of the small boxes that needed to be checked to launch the ministry in the best possible way. Have you ever tried to do something well and forgotten some of the small things? Have you ever been unable to get a job or a promotion because a few small things were not done right? Have you been trying to repair your marriage or your relationships with your children, but you haven't really dealt with the "small" thing that happened in the past? Do you know you could do so much more, but others won't give you the chance because you lack a certification or a degree or particular membership? The small stuff mattered to Jesus. He is our example.

5. John Baptized Jesus

Jesus walked into the cold and muddy waters of the Jordan which symbolized Kingdom readiness. Standing waist deep in the water, John might have said something like: "Are you anxiously awaiting the coming kingdom of God?" or "Are you ready to be a part of the coming kingdom of God?"

Holding Jesus by the tunic in front and in back, John thrust Jesus forward into the muddy water, surrounding Him in the symbol of readiness for the Kingdom. Was Jesus ready for the Kingdom? Of course! He had been ready for centuries, even millennia. Now after all that time, here He was on the eve of the long-awaited Kingdom of God.

There was far more going on in eternal dimensions than we have recorded in the gospels. This was the beginning of the salvation of mankind. Remember that angels long to look into salvation. On the night of Jesus' birth, a whole armada of angels burst out in praise to God after the announcement to the shepherds. Imagine what the angels were experiencing as they watched this long-awaited drama actually move to center stage. No longer would the payment for mankind's sins be shrouded in the symbol of animal sacrifice. No longer would we see through the pieces and proportions of the tabernacle. The real thing was here on earth beginning His ministry. The Lamb of God was presenting Himself to Israel and to the world.

6. Jesus Prayed

Jesus came up from the waters and paused to pray. He offered Himself up as God's instrument -- a complete sacrifice for the commencement of the Kingdom. We don't know what exactly He prayed, but we can take clues from other prayers He spoke or taught:

> *Therefore, when He comes into the world, He says,*
> *"Sacrifice and offering You have not desired,*
> *But a body You have prepared for Me;*
> *In whole burnt offerings and sacrifices for sin*

> *You have taken no pleasure.*
> *"Then I said, 'Behold, I have come (in the scroll of the book it is written of Me) to do Your will, O God.'"* (Hebrews 10:5-7)

> *"Pray, then, in this way:*
> *'Our Father who is in heaven,*
> *Hallowed be Your name.*
> *Your kingdom come.*
> *Your will be done,*
> *On earth as it is in heaven.'"* (Matthew 6:9, 10)

On the eve of His death for the sins of the world, Jesus later said, "For this I came into the world." His baptism was the beginning of this cosmic drama. God veiled in flesh was living a perfect life on this earth, and His ministry of showing Himself was beginning. We cannot comprehend the depth of prayer between Jesus, the Father, and the Spirit. Jesus was completely dependent on the Father and the Spirit to live this life and complete this ministry. He was really communicating with God.

7. God the Holy Spirit Broke into the Scene

Jesus prayed on the bank of the river. While focusing wholly on God and the coming Kingdom, God unexpectedly broke into the scene by opening the curtain that separates the eternal dimensions from ours. This had happened before to Ezekiel (Ezekiel 1:1), and also to Stephen (Acts 7:56), Paul (2 Corinthians 12:1-4), and John (Revelation 4:1, 11:19, 19:11).

The Bible describes it as a white blur - something like a dove that came down out of a sort of inter-universal hole. It landed on Jesus and stayed there. This was the promised signal John was waiting for that would assure Him that Jesus was the King. This descending, white, dove-like blur also spiritually empowered Jesus in some new way for the grueling ministry ahead. Without this special anointing by the Holy Spirit, Jesus in His human nature could not have completed the task before Him. Jesus was in this way the second Adam. He was perfectly dependent upon the Spirit of God, doing what God wanted. He is the perfect role model and example to us.

The Scriptures are clear in Philippines 2:5-10 that Jesus laid aside the use of His own deity in order to show us how to live. He lived as a spirit-empowered human even though He was God Himself. The life of a human was always meant to be a spirit-dependent life. The life of faith consists of waiting upon and listening for the whisper of God. He has not sent us here to do our best. He wants us to invite the Spirit in and live our life as a spiritual work in process. Jesus did this and His anointing and empowering by the Spirit at this point allowed the ministry that followed to take place.

This "kenosis," a self-emptying or self-renunciation of His own will to become entirely receptive to God's, is described in Scripture:

Have this attitude in yourselves which was also in Christ Jesus, who, although He existed in the form of God, did not regard equality with God a thing to be grasped, but emptied Himself, taking the form of a bond-servant, and being made in the likeness of a man.
(Philippians 2:5-7)

Scripture also tells us that everything Jesus did was by the empowering of the Holy Spirit. It seems clear from this passage that if the power of the Lord were not present from the Father and the Spirit, Jesus would not have healed on that day. Yes, He could have healed out of His own divinity, but then He would not have been the perfect man.

One day He was teaching; and there were some Pharisees and teachers of the law sitting there who had come from every village of Galilee and Judea and from Jerusalem; and the power of the Lord was present for Him to perform healing. (Luke 5:17)

This is another reference demonstrating that it was God the Father and God the Spirit that worked through Jesus while He was on the earth. This is the way that God wants to work through us. He does not want us to ask Him to bless our plans and goals, but He wants to empower us to accomplish His plans and goals.

Do you not believe that I am in the Father, and the Father is in Me? The words that I say to you I do not speak on My own initiative, but the Father abiding in Me does His works. (John 14:10)

Jesus tells us that He is ever waiting for the Spirit of God to direct Him. The relationship of dependence and submission was absolute. This is the model for our life in Christ. We wait upon Him.

And He who sent Me is with Me; He has not left Me alone, for I always do the things that are pleasing to Him. (John 8:29)

Let me also add that Jesus' life was not a robotic life where instructions from God were given for putting on shoes or eating food. Jesus the man thought, played, laughed, decided, and related; but He was always ready to do what God directed Him to do. God has given us a brain and we should use it, but we must lean hard into His plans for us.

God seeks to also empower us for service on His behalf through His Spirit. He baptizes us into the body of Christ. He makes us to drink of the same Spirit. He gives us gifts. He gives us ministries in which to participate. He guides us in how to live and how to minister to others. God adds these and many other elements to our life when we become Christians. Jesus was anointed for His ministry, and God has a ministry for each of us that He has likewise empowered and anointed us in order to accomplish.

8. God the Father Speaks

Then a voice *booms* out of this inter-dimensional hole. There is no introduction as to who the speaker is, so we find out who is speaking by what is said. It is fascinating what the voice says because we see from Scripture that there are really two different messages -- one to John and one to Jesus. To John it says, *"This is My Beloved Son, in Whom I am well-pleased."* (Matthew 3:16-17). And to Jesus, *"You are My beloved Son, in You I am well-pleased."* (Mark 1:11). There are only three words that are different between these two messages. The voice could have repeated itself once to John, then once to Jesus. Or it could have spoken to Jesus and translated the words somehow differently to John. That wouldn't be beyond the scope of our powerful God.

We know by the content of the message that this is the voice of God the Father. This is the *voice of Yahweh* speaking into our world and giving encouragement, blessing, and strength. Abraham heard this voice, as did Moses, Joshua, Isaiah, Daniel, Peter, James, John, and Paul.

The Father is well pleased in the Son. Jesus had lived on planet earth for approximately thirty years in seclusion, listening to His earthly father and His Heavenly Father. God was pleased by this non-famous life. In our day and age we are often too much in a hurry to make an impact, and we do not have enough solitude and preparation to make a good or lasting impact. Don't despise the times of preparation. Move when God says it is time even if your culture or your personality says you are waiting too long.

Jesus Christ, by His willing submission to the plan of the Father, became the channel for the love, pleasure, and delight of God to flow to man. In fact, He is the *only* channel. Because of Christ, God's unlimited love, peace, grace, and mercy is opened to frail, feeble, sinful, and rebellious men. What an incredible canal Christ dug with His own flesh that would carry the love of God!

Delighting in Jesus

Jesus waited for God to have all the pieces prepared before launching into His worldwide ministry. Does God have you waiting for the launch of something? It is amazing that Jesus waited for thirty years before this world-changing ministry began. He knew from the time He was twelve that He had to be about His Father's business. Imagine Him in His twenties still hammering, sawing, and chiseling wood tables and chairs while He waited for the right time.

Most Christians are waiting for something. They need a door to open, a job to be offered, a graduation to occur, someone to retire, someone to help them, their children to come, their children to leave. During these times of waiting we should be strengthening our love for God and our love for others. It is this preparation time that will allow for the impact that we know is our destiny.

Right now, think about what are you waiting for God to do in your life?

How are you spending your time while you wait?

What do you need to learn, develop, or accomplish during this waiting period?

It is normal to be waiting. Those who wait well are able to see God in the waiting. We know of only one time that Jesus chafed in His waiting for the mission to begin -- when He was twelve. Learn to explore other parts of your world than just the part you want to start. Too many people let the rest of their life atrophy while they are waiting to get married, graduate college, get their dream job, or have children. Don't let this happen to you. Become the fully developed person that you can be while you are waiting. It will become apparent that God did not waste the time of waiting if you take full advantage of it.

Jesus' baptism was a small, simple symbol, but it was something important to accomplish. We all have these kinds of seemingly small tasks to accomplish in order to be able to really live the life God has for us. Sometimes these are tasks that we don't want to do because they seem like a hassle. Why can't the powers that be just give you the thing you deserve without this little thing? Sometimes these are called "incompletes," and we must go back and finish these tasks before we can move on. Sometimes the "small" thing will take years to accomplish, and then it can fade into the background of your life.

Are their some small tasks that you need to do before you can move forward significantly in your life? What are they? (For example, graduation from college, taking a particular exam, certification of some kind, updating your look, asking permission before getting married, paying off a debt, making a budget, making a business plan, etc.)

Are there some incompletes in your life that you need to go back and finish before you are ready to move forward in your life? (Debts to pay, relationships, wounds, offenses, filing back taxes, etc.)

Are there any "small" things that will fade into the background once they are completed but require time and money to complete right now? (Schooling, certifications, licenses, or an appearance at a certain event, etc.)

Jesus' baptism was a spiritual symbol of His devotion to God as well as His identification with the Kingdom of God. God asks us to take a stand for Him publically through baptism, also. We become a Christian through admission of our need

The Baptism of Jesus

for the Savior and through our invitation to let Him come run our lives. When this happens we should also be baptized. Baptism in this sense is a picture of three things about our life: First, that we are willing to totally identify God as three-in-one or Triune (Matthew 28:18-20). Second, that we are willing to die to our old way of life and live responding to a new master, the Lord, rather than our flesh (Romans 6:1-16). Third, that we are wanting God to scrub us clean from our sins just like getting into a bathtub with soap would scrub us clean from our dirt (1 Peter 3:21).

Have you ever been baptized as a Christian adult? This is the way to publically declare that you are a Christian. It announces to the world and eternity that you are serious about being a Christian. Tell your pastor that you want to be baptized.

Jesus' baptism was also a time for Him to be empowered for the mission He was to accomplish. Jesus walked in complete dependence upon the Father and the Holy Spirit during His time on earth. This is the way to live the Christian life. Move toward dependence upon God the Father, God the Son, and God the Holy Spirit. God has and will empower you for serving Him. When we become a Christian, God the Holy Spirit empowers us for service for Him. He does this by residing in and with us, giving us at least one spiritual gift, providing us a ministry to use this gift in some way, and guiding us to live for Him. Let me help you move toward accomplishing your mission for God just as Jesus accomplished His.

God's mission for all of our lives is relational. Jesus tells us that the two greatest commands are about relationships --

loving God and loving others. Each of us has some good works that we can do (Ephesians 2:10) to move that objective forward. Not everyone will be receptive to your love and help though. God's love through you may be directed towards masses of people, or it may be directed just at your family and friends. The world is after money, power, fame, and pleasure; but God wants us to carry His message of relational repair to everyone who will listen. God went to all the trouble of sending His Son Jesus to live in this world and then give up His life voluntarily so that our relationship with God could be repaired (John 3:16).

What mission is God sending you on?

What relationships need to be repaired in your world?

Who do you know that might be open to repairing their relationship with God through Jesus' sacrifice?

Chapter 2
The Temptation of Christ

Key Verses

Matthew 4:1-14 - *Then Jesus was led up by the Spirit into the wilderness to be tempted by the Devil. And after He had fasted forty days and forty nights, He then became hungry. And the Tempter came and said to Him, "If you are the Son of God, command that these stones become bread...but He answered and said, "It is written, 'man shall not live on bread alone, but on every word that proceeds out of the mouth of God.'" Then the Devil took Him into the holy city; and He had Him stand on the pinnacle of the temple, and said to Him, "If you are the Son of God throw yourself down; for it is written, 'He will give His angels charge concerning you'; and 'On their hands they will bear you up, lest you strike your foot against a stone.'" Jesus said to Him, "On the other hand, it is written, 'You shall not put the Lord your God to the test.'" Again, the Devil took Him to a very high mountain and showed Him all the kingdoms of the world, and their glory; and he said to Him, "All these things will I give you, if you fall down and worship me." Then Jesus said to Him, "Be gone, Satan! For it is written, 'You shall worship the Lord your God, and serve Him only.'" Then the Devil left Him; and behold, angels came and began to minister to Him.*

Luke 4:1-13 - *"And Jesus, full of the Holy Spirit, returned from the Jordan and was led about by the Spirit in the wilderness for forty days, being tempted by the Devil. And He ate nothing during those days; and when they had ended, He became hungry. And the Devil said to Him, "If you are the Son of God, tell this stone to become bread." And Jesus answered Him, "It is written, 'Man shall not live on bread alone.'" And he led Him up and showed Him all the kingdoms of the world in a moment of time. And the Devil said to Him, "I will give you all this domain and its glory; for it has been handed over to me, and I give it to whomever I wish. Therefore if you worship before me, it shall all be yours." And Jesus answered and said to Him, "It is written, 'You shall worship the Lord your God and serve Him only.'" And he led Him to Jerusalem and had Him stand on the pinnacle of the temple, and said to Him, "If you are the Son of God, throw yourself down from here; for it is written, 'He will give His angels charge concerning you to guard you,' and, 'On their hands they will bear you up, lest you strike your foot against a stone.'" And Jesus answered and said to Him, "It is said, 'You shall not put the Lord your God to the test.'" And when the Devil had finished every temptation, he departed from Him until an opportune time."*

The following account of Jesus' encounter with the Devil is very instructive for our lives. Jesus is the supreme example of how to live a life dependent upon God. He demonstrated that aspect of His life to an extreme degree here in His encounter with the Devil. It would be instructive to have a detailed record of what God the Father and the Spirit were communicating with Jesus the God/man during the first forty days of this fast, but we are not told about those details. Instead, the Scriptures tell us about Jesus' direct interaction with Satan. Satan slinked into this interaction right after the forty-day fast. There is no introduction of Satan; he just started right in with the manipulative work he is so good at deploying. Jesus did not defeat Satan as God (that would have been too easy). Rather, He defeated him as the perfect man using the tools that we, as Christians, have available to us. There are eight basic spiritual weapons available to all believers that the Apostle Paul detailed later in his letter to the Ephesians:

1. Truth
2. Righteousness
3. Peace
4. Faith/risk
5. Salvation/a way of escape
6. The word of God
7. Prayer
8. Alertness

Each time in this episode, Jesus counteracted Lucifer's attack with the sixth of the basic spiritual weapons. This will be very instructive in battling temptation in your own life.

The Story Detailed

Following His baptism, Jesus completely surrendered to the power of the Holy Spirit and was led up into the wilderness. Legend tells us that the Spirit led Jesus to the region of Mount Quarantana -- the wilderness on the opposite side of the Jordan River. Rather than leading Jesus back to civilization, the Spirit led Jesus away into greater isolation and seclusion.

In order to move into public ministry as God's perfect servant, the last hurdle that Jesus needed to face was overcoming the *test of temptation*. He had faced the *test of waiting* (Moses had failed). He had faced the *test of submission* (to the smallest of details). He had been *empowered by the Holy Spirit*. Now all He had left to do was to resist the Tempter. Would He rely completely on the power of the Spirit to overcome temptation or do it some other way?

It was critical to God's plan for salvation that Jesus win this battle for if Christ were to have depended in any way on His own attributes of divinity, then His example and ministry would be over. Even worse, He would have committed sin and plunged the world into destruction. In other words, Jesus could not put one ounce of dependence upon His own flesh, or it would have been sin just like it is for us.

Jesus fasted and did not eat anything for forty days. Many scholars believe that this was a supernatural fast where Jesus neither ate nor drank anything. This would have been like the fast Moses endured during his interaction with God on Mt. Sinai. Other scholars believe that while Jesus did not eat anything, He probably drank water. The Bible doesn't state what He did with His time, but we know that He was somehow about the Father's business. Whether it was to get from the Father the complete layout of His ministry or to concentrate more fully on the work of the Spirit within Him, we do not know.

As you might imagine, Jesus was very hungry at the end of this forty-day period. There are two types of hunger human beings experience:

> 1. An uneasy sensation occasioned by a lack of food.
> 2. An urgent need for food.

The first is a psychological impulse brought on by the interruption of normal food-intake routines. The second is an intense physical need for food before the body melts down. Jesus was suffering from this type of hunger. His body intensely needed food or else it was going to shut down completely.

When Jesus was at the weakest possible moment, the Tempter came and plied his trade. This was the point when He had the greatest possible chance of thinking that there must be a better way to save the world -- the desire to pick up His own divinity and powers (His own weapons) would have been tempting. After all, He was dying physically!

The Scriptures record three names for the Devil in this narrative:

> 1. *The Devil,* meaning *"The Slanderer."* He always comes to us this way -- questioning, accusing, taunting, and getting us to feel condemned in our person. He tries to get us to question our basic nature and to try something stupid so that he can prove we are who we are.

> 2. *The Tempter,* which means one who entices us to do wrong by promise of pleasure or gain. He always holds out the promise of future reward in order to entice us to do evil at the moment that we would not naturally consider doing such a thing.

> 3. *Satan,* which means "adversary" or "opponent." He is our opponent. He stands against us no matter what we do right.

Notice the wilderness wandering and temptation account lasted for a specific number of days, a set period of time. Jesus probably did not know how long this would last, but He knew that this evil day would come to an end eventually. The Apostle Paul tells us in Ephesians 6:10-18 that there will be an evil day and we must stand firm. We don't know how long it will last; but we must not give into seductions, opposition, or destruction of the Devil. When it comes to temptation, it is always too early to give in.

The First Temptation

In the midst of Jesus' extreme weariness, the Devil came as the Tempter to entice Him into sacrificing future glory for present gain. He also came as the Devil slandering Christ with the question, "If you are the Son of God..." He knew very well who Jesus was, but he was taunting Him into trying to prove it by His own testimony.

Notice that the Devil did not introduce himself in any of the exchanges before us. He is only identified by the content of his message and the actions he took. He essentially was saying, "Prove to me that you are the Son of God." In actuality it would not have been proven to anyone. The Devil would only have asked for more proof and Jesus already knew who He was.

The temptation centered seemingly on bread, but the real issue was whether Jesus was going to use his own powers or remain dependent upon the Holy Spirit. Jesus could have clearly turned the stones into bread. To remain spiritual, though, Jesus could not use His divinity just as we cannot use our flesh. The energizing principle for the spiritual man must be the Holy Spirit of the Living God.

Bread is the staple of the Middle Eastern diet. It was the main part of every meal. All the other things were thought of as accessories to the bread. We tend to think this way about steak or meat. The meal is only a snack if there is no meat.

The Devil comes to us and tempts us to rely upon our smarts, our cunning, our shortcuts, and our schemes to accomplish something that God has given us as a goal. Satan tries to get us to believe that it is okay to accomplish the will of God by our own power without relying on God. This is what he was trying to get Jesus to do. In Jesus' case it was a little different because Jesus was God and He could do anything. But if Jesus had unleashed his deity to provide for Himself, then He would have ceased to be the perfect man and our Savior. This was the Devil's plan to derail the salvation that Jesus came to provide.

The Devil's suggestion to change the stones into bread was a really stupid idea if you analyze it carefully. Having just fasted for forty days, Jesus could not have handled any type of solid food without becoming violently sick. He needed broth to come off the fast properly and easily. Bread was merely a psychological ploy designed to get Christ's mouth watering. He couldn't have digested what He would have created if He had followed the Devil's lie. Like all of Satan's promises, they are false and usually detrimental much in the same way a thirteen-year-old girl dresses up to attract men, the gambler risks his meager earnings to have great wealth, or the sixteen-year-old runs away from home to find freedom.

Interestingly, it is suggested that there were many stones in that region that were round and looked like a loaf of bread, further enticing Jesus to succumb to the temptation.

Jesus' Reply

Jesus faced Satan not as God but as a man dependent upon the Spirit of the Living God. He was armed only with the same weapons that we as mortal men have. As God He could have commanded that Satan be gone or banished him to hell immediately for trying to tempt Him. But He was willing to face Satan with only simple weapons in order that He might be a complete example to us on how to defeat Satan.

Jesus immediately quoted from Scripture. He did not address who He was speaking to ("Satan, why should I listen to anything you say?"), but knowing Scripture so well He selected the passage in the Old Testament that dealt with a similar situation.

The children of Israel lacked bread and were grumbling because they were hungry. God gave them manna, but He let them know that they should look to Him for life, not to bread or food (Deuteronomy 8:2-3).

Bread just sustains life; it does not create it. God gives life and it is important to stay dependent on the right source. The words of God contain life, energy like little Pac-Man dots. It was the word of God that produced life, bread, flesh, and everything else in the first place. Notice how Jesus did not reply:

Personal:	Satan, I know it's you; get out of here.
Scientific:	I cannot possibly digest bread; ridiculous!
Knowledge:	You doubt that I am the Son of God.
Socratic:	What do you mean by command, bread, Son of God?

The Holy Spirit prompted Jesus with a verse of Scripture just like He does for us in our moments of temptation. "Man shall not live by bread alone, but by every word that proceeds out of the mouth of God." Whenever we hear a verse of Scripture placed in our soul in the midst of a struggle with the Devil, it is God's strategy to defeat him and should be repeated out loud. Jesus quoted this verse and let its power and God's protection take care of the Devil.

The Word of God releases life only when it is heard, understood, and acted upon. God's Word must become our life in order to receive the life it offers. We must do it, not just treat it as a magical formula or supernatural hocus-pocus.

Now if Satan ever asks you to change stones into bread or steaks, then you will know what to reply! This would be ridiculous since we don't have the ability to do that. But by relying on the flesh, we can change all kinds of things into money, wealth, food, or material comforts through stealing, lying, cheating, gambling, sex, alcohol, etc. Do not give into the promises of the Devil or depend upon the flesh for the conversion of these assets.

What's amazing is that when Jesus quoted the Scriptural answer, the temptation immediately moved on to the next type. The Devil did not push that answer or ask questions about it. He knew he was defeated. Jesus won this battle, but the Devil just moved on to the next strategy.

The Second Temptation

During the second temptation Satan took Jesus to the pinnacle of the temple. We are not told the method of transportation or the reason why Jesus allowed Satan to take Him anywhere in the first place!

The pinnacle of the temple was some 326' to 450' above the valley floor below. One interesting note is that this is the same pinnacle that James, the Lord's brother, was thrown from and killed during the later persecution of the church.

Again the Devil came as a slanderer, questioning whether Jesus was really the Son of God. This time he questioned the Father's protection of the Son. He seemed again to be saying that Jesus needed to prove Himself to him as if Satan's approval was important.

The Devil's strategy was to get Jesus to try to manipulate God on Jesus' behalf. This temptation was designed to force God the Father to publically show support for Jesus, so the world-wide program of redemption could begin on a sped-up timetable. God, however, has His own timetable. God also will not be put into a manipulated situation. Too many people have fallen for this kind of temptation: "God, you must heal my wife because she is such a servant of yours." "If you don't (...), I will not love you or serve you." I heard one man tell me those words as he harbored a deep bitterness toward God for taking his wife to heaven. He had been manipulated into believing that he could box God into making just one choice. Some people listen to the Devil tempt them to manipulate God into answering prayers for jobs, relationships, promotions, homes, or money. He is trying to set you up to be disappointed with God if He doesn't do it your way or meet your expectations. God is God and He will do what He wants when He wants. Yes, sometimes He responds to our prayers, but we are never in charge of God.

The Devil quoted from Scripture: Psalm 91:1,2. If it's any surprise to you that Satan knows Scripture, it shouldn't be. He is a master at stating Scripture but for his own twisted purposes. It is important to note that Jesus does not squabble with interpretation but goes to the heart of the matter: "You want me to test God?"

When the Devil comes in our lives, he will not identify himself; so we must understand the question, temptation, or whatever the case may be from the standpoint of what he is trying to get us to do. For example, he might plant a thought like, "If God really loves you as a Christian, wouldn't he have to heal your child?" Or how about, "If God was really on your side, then how come all these bad things keep happening to you?" His main goal and purpose is to cast doubt, stir up division, and separate us so that we'll stop following God.

Jesus' Reply
Jesus saw right through what the Devil was trying to do. As humans we are not to try to manipulate God. God will act when and where He wants to. How did Jesus know what the Devil was doing? Most likely it was because of the Scripture that God the Father and the Spirit whispered to Him. Jesus put the Devil down with this one quote from Scripture.

Hundreds of feet above the valley floor, the battle was quickly over. Luke's gospel says, "You shall not force a test on the Lord your God" (Luke 4:12; Deuteronomy 6:16). When God brings to mind Scripture in the midst of a temptation or encounter with the Devil, He is trying to help us understand the nature of the temptation. Jesus' repeating of this Scripture was the clear indication that He understood the nature of the temptation.

Just as the teacher does not allow the students to write the questions, we should not put God to the test. If God allowed these types of tests, then He would be led around by our promises of service for His passing our tests. All kinds of people do this today and the tests never end. It sounds like: "Make my life great, and I'll serve you." They intend to make God prove that He is God. If He passes, He is God, and if He doesn't, then He isn't. Other tests that people put in front of God include:

- No blood transfusions
- No medical attention
- Snake handling
- On-demand healing
- Material possessions

Embrace the reality that God is God and you are not. We can pray and we can serve, but we will not put God in a situation where we are commanding Him. Let God direct you in the midst of the spiritual attacks that the Devil brings against you. Listen for the whispers of His will. Be ready to use the spiritual weapons of truth, righteousness, peace, risk, ways of escape, Scripture, prayer, and alertness rather than trying to defeat the Devil through your own willpower or your clever ideas.

The Third Temptation
Notice that the Devil is relentless. He flowed right away into the next temptation. There was no indication that this temptation would be based upon the last one. He just rolled on to the next area of potential weakness to probe. In the same way the Devil will do this to us. We are tempted by financial pressures to do something dumb and just as we are in the midst of that, our sister gets sick. We are tempted to get mad at God and just as we are coming out of that, we are tempted by a promotion that would cause us to compromise a little of our ethics. The Devil is relentless. He probes and piles on when you are down. He does not fight fair. Expect this process and the weariness that comes with it. You can win with the weapons that Jesus has given you, just as Jesus won with the weapons that the Father and the Spirit gave Him.

In this final temptation the Devil took Jesus to a very high mountain. It is not suggested directly that being on top of the mountain was what provided the incredible view Satan presented to Jesus. This just seemed to be the place where Satan likely gave Jesus a vision of the kingdoms of the world and their glory. Realize that the Devil can give visions that seem wonderful and spectacular.

Imagine what Jesus must have seen:
- Spectacular palaces
- Exotic women of different lands

- Extravagant riches and opulence
- Rich and desirable foods
- Pleasures of a thousand worlds and cultures

Notice that Jesus did not debate the truth with the claims of the Devil. Some have suggested that Satan really is in charge of the dominions of the world (Ephesians 2:2, Daniel 9, Hebrews 2). But even if this were true, then it would only be for a season. He won't control it forever. The people who give in to the Devil's alluring song have not thought this out long term. The claims of the Devil will not stay true -- sexual pleasures fade with age, the happiness that money can buy diminishes quickly, and desires that seem to completely satisfy are like a cancer, eating away at your insides. God's promises are small and get larger (Psalm 37:1-11), but Satan's promises start big and get smaller.

Again, when analyzed correctly, we see this was another stupid temptation. It was presented as a way to become the king of mankind without having to endure the cross. But Jesus' mission involved setting up a rival kingdom with Satan and defeating it for world rulership. How ridiculous to believe you can set up a rival kingdom by joining your rival! Again, this temptation didn't pass the test of common sense. As with all of the Devil's suggestions, it was unworkable in the way he presented it.

But Jesus didn't fight it this way. Think for a moment if Jesus had given into this temptation. The implications of this scenario are mind-bending! Satan's suggestion would have actually placed Jesus as the Antichrist. If Jesus had deserted His mission as the Savior and Messiah of mankind, it would have done more than put Him in the position of "satanic ruler of the world." It would have put the second person of the Trinity in rebellion with other members of the Godhead! The One who upholds all things by the word of His power would have been at odds with the prime unity, God. There would have been a rift of destruction at the core of all creation that would have destroyed the very fabric of the universe in which we live. What Satan does not realize is that for Jesus to do what he suggested would have meant the material universe, including Satan, would cease to exist as it is presently constituted -- if at all.

This is the way that Satan's suggestions always operate. He promises the trapped housewife that she can escape her boredom with an affair, but he does not let her know that it will cost her security, the love of her children, destruction of friendships, emotional upheavals, and other irreparable damages. Usually it is too late when people discover that, yes, you can have what Satan promised but everything else in your world will be damaged, if not completely destroyed.

Let's be clear. Satan was offering Jesus a shortcut to His goal of becoming the ruler of the world. It was the right goal (Jesus will be ruler of the world openly), but it was the wrong way to achieve it. The Devil will come to us and offer to help us achieve a particular goal. But we will only have to lie, cheat, steal, and/or compromise in some way to achieve it. Surely he will tell you that the accomplishment of the goal is worth a little bending of the rules. But it is not true. If you have to break the rules to accomplish a righteous goal, then it is no longer a righteous goal -- it will accomplish something else altogether.

We have to be careful about who and what we worship.
Worship is ascribing worth and value above what is proper for that object or person. It is crucial that we establish the relative worth of an object or person or else we might be engaged in worship. When someone places more value on their car than their wife, it is rightly said that they are worshipping their car. If we put more value on our children, our money, or our home than God, then we are moving into the realms of false worship. Anything placed above God is false worship. There are lesser gods who often demand the wrong amount of attention. We can worship a thing for a very short time and then find something else for our affection to land on. The Devil has very little trouble with us on this one. We give in so easily. Every new purchase seems to be the god for that week. Each champion in professional or college sports becomes a god for a year. The value we give to them is way out of proportion to their importance in our lives. God is a jealous god and demands our full devotion (Deuteronomy 4:24, 5:7).

Jesus' Reply
Jesus ultimately dismissed Satan for who he is -- the Adversary. He'd had enough. This was the first time that Jesus used this term for His enemy. Satan exposed his real purpose -- the desire to have worship and honor. He is the adversary in that he opposes the ultimate goal of man which is to worship and enjoy God only.

Jesus finally dismissed Satan when we would have thought He would have done it much earlier. He seemed content to allow the Devil to have his little game until he stepped on the one thing that Jesus could not allow -- *diminishing the glory of*

God. Unfortunately as God's people we are not more zealous for the glory of the Holy God. We seem far more upset at the Devil's enticements that only prove to be destructive and deceptive. This is proof that we really do not have God's thoughts. He is far more concerned about His glory than we could ever imagine. Isaiah 42:8 says, *"I am the Lord, that is My name; I will not give My glory to another, nor My praise to graven images."*

This is the first of Jesus' replies that hints at impatience or anger. Jesus is appalled at the idea that God's value structure would be tampered with and especially that anyone would suggest tampering with God's place as Number One. Didn't Jesus say that the greatest commandment is to "Love God with all your heart, soul, mind, and strength"? We see here by His emotional reaction that He believes every word of this commandment.

Jesus quoted from Deuteronomy 6:13, where Moses was instructing the new generation of Israelites that the most important concept to grasp was the place of God in their society and personal lives. He is Number One. Because we as a society, and even as individual Christians, have been putting all kinds of things in God's place, we have a completely topsy-turvy society. It is God who tells us that families are more important than jobs. It is God who tells us that children are more important than hobbies. It is God who tells us that harmony is more important than always being right. When we don't put God as the most important object of affection, then we are cast adrift on a sea of relativity with each man deciding for Himself the value of things. This leaves us incredibly susceptible to the siren songs of the Devil's false values.

It is a shame that when Jesus mentions worshiping God, many Christians automatically think of singing. Worship is so much more than singing in services on Sunday. Jesus explains there are two halves to worship:

- Direct worship - the worshiper ascribes glory, honor, value, and worth to God directly through voice, song, action, thought, drawing, and writing. Through these we can get caught up in the overwhelming awesomeness of God.

- Indirect worship - the worshiper uses every ability, talent, gift, and object to reflect the glory of God. Everything he does, says, writes, etc., is designed for God even though its more immediate recipient might be someone else.

Notice Jesus said that no matter who you work for or serve in any capacity, you are to really only be serving the Lord. All things that the Christian does is to be done for the Lord, and if the Lord cannot be boss of that thing, then the Christian cannot do it.

Jesus 3, Satan 0
Matthew's gospel tells us that the Devil had been thwarted. He tried to tempt Jesus three different ways to get Him to desert His mission. His master plan with all of the trappings had been quickly pushed aside. After the third temptation, the Devil finally left Jesus, thus ending the forty-day fast. He was beaten with only the simple weapons of Spirit-dependency and Scripture. Jesus never deserted His mission or drew upon His own unique ability to defeat the Devil. Instead, He

became our supreme example and showed us the way to send the Devil packing in our lives.

Luke's gospel records that the Devil didn't permanently retreat from Jesus though; he just pulled back for another opportune moment. Jesus would face this foe again and again in His ministry. Each time it was with the Spirit's permission, and each time it was at a weak (or supposedly weak) moment. But the prescription had been set -- the Devil was defeated by dependence on the Spirit and use of the Scriptures. Although we are never told of another direct attack of Satan like this one, it is probable that they did occur. For instance, we do know that Jesus was attacked by Satan dressed in the garb of the Apostle Peter in Matthew 16.

There will be times when you are not under spiritual attack, just as Jesus had a respite from the onslaught of the enemy. But Jesus' victory over temptation did not last forever and neither will any of yours. Until you enter God's eternal glory, there is no one thing that will get Satan off your back for good.

After the Devil left, we are told that angels appeared to minister to Jesus and supplied what He needed to regain His strength and energy. It is amazing that God waited this long to send them, but He knew just when to rescue His beloved son. It is important to realize that the angels did not appear because Jesus was God; rather it was because the Father loved Him. The Father loves us, too, and if we need this kind of help, then we will receive it. Church history is replete with stories of men and women who have received supernatural help just when they needed it.

Delighting in Jesus

Just as the Lord was tempted, attacked, and opposed by the Devil, we too will be tempted, attacked, and opposed by the spiritual forces of wickedness. We will need to be ready to respond with the spiritual weapons that God has provided. These are called the Armor of God in Ephesians. Jesus only used the sixth piece of the armor to defeat the Devil in these encounters, but He shows us in other places the use of the other pieces.

As I work my way through this basic list of Spiritual weapons, God always prompts me about which piece(s) of the armor to use and what I need to know to utilize it (them) in that situation. Jesus was the perfect servant of God and was prompted to use the sixth piece of armor all three times in this episode. The Devil will not come after you with the pinnacle of the temple test; but he will bring temptations, manipulations, lies, fears, and doubts which can be defeated by putting on the full armor of God and resisting him just as Jesus did.

I believe that Jesus allowed the Father and the Holy Spirit to guide His responses to the Devil, so we should also ask God (Father, Son, and Holy Spirit) which pieces of the armor He wants us to use and how to do it. This is spiritual business and requires us to tune in to God's direction.

1. In this spiritual exercise it is helpful to first identify any areas of temptation in your life. Are you being plagued by some of the same temptations Jesus faced? What sort of

temptations could you be going through right now? Fear, doubt, shortcuts, lies, anger, bitterness, sorcery...?

2. When I believe I am facing the Devil or one of his demons -- either personally or when I am working with another person who is under attack -- I go right down through the basic armor of God for the answers (Ephesians 6:10-18). As you pray over this list of the spiritual weapons, let God guide you to which weapons He wants you to begin using right away in your own personal battles with the Devil. Write down what God wants you to do and begin to win by resisting the Devil in your life.

- What truth needs to be known or used to defeat this spiritual attack?

- What righteous behavior needs to be known or done to defeat this spiritual attack?

- What peace strategies need to be employed to defeat this spiritual attack?

- What trust in God, expression of faith, or God-ordained risk needs to be attempted to defeat this spiritual attack?

- What way of escape needs to be taken to defeat this spiritual attack?

- What verse of Scripture needs to be known or quoted to defeat this spiritual attack?

- What prayers need to be prayed to defeat this spiritual attack?

- What precautions or alertness needs to be put in place to defeat this spiritual attack?

To get a more comprehensive understanding of these spiritual weapons, take a look at my book, *Secrets of God's Armor*, at www.ptlb.com.

Chapter 3
Jesus Visits His Hometown

Key Verses

Matthew 13:53-58 - *And it came about that when Jesus had finished these parables, He departed from there. And coming to His hometown He began teaching them in their synagogue, so that they became astonished, and said, "Where did this man get this wisdom, and these miraculous powers? Is not this the carpenter's son? Is not His mother called Mary, and His brothers, James and Joseph and Simon and Judas? "And His sisters, are they not all with us? Where then did this man get all these things?" And they took offense at him. But Jesus said to them, "A prophet is not without honor except in his hometown, and in his own household." And He did not do many miracles there because of their unbelief.*

Mark 6:1-6 - *And He went out from there, and He came into His hometown; and His disciples followed Him. And when the Sabbath had come, He began to teach in the synagogue: and the many listeners were astonished, saying, "Where did this man get these things, and what is this wisdom given to him, and such miracles as these performed by His hands? Is not this the carpenter, the son of Mary, and brother of James, and Joseph, and Judas, and Simon? Are not His sisters here with us?" And they took offense at him. And Jesus said to them, "A prophet is not without honor except in his home town and among his own relatives and in his own household." And He could do no miracle there except that He laid His hands* upon a few sick people and healed them. And He wondered at their unbelief. And He was going around the villages teaching.

Luke 4:16-30 - *And He came to Nazareth, where He had been brought up; and as was His custom, He entered the synagogue on the Sabbath, and stood up to read. And the book of the prophet Isaiah was handed to Him. And He opened the book, and found the place where it was written "The Spirit of the Lord is upon me because He anointed me to preach the gospel to the poor. He has sent me to proclaim release to the captives, and recovery of sight to the blind, To set free those who are downtrodden, to proclaim the favorable year of the Lord." And He closed the book, and gave it back to the attendant, and sat down; and the eyes of all in the synagogue were fixed upon Him. And He began to say to them, "Today this Scripture has been fulfilled in your hearing." And all were speaking well of Him, and wondering at the gracious words which were falling from His lips; and they were saying, "Is this not Joseph's son?" And He said to them, "No doubt you will quote this proverb to Me, 'Physician, heal yourself! Whatever we heard was done at Capernaum, do here in your home town as well.'" And He said, "Truly I say to you, no prophet is welcome in his home town. But I say to you in truth, there were many widows in Israel in the days of Elijah, when the sky was shut up for three years and six months, when a great famine came over all the land; and yet Elijah was sent to none of them, but only to Zarephath, in the land of Sidon, to a woman who was a widow. And there were many lepers in Israel in the time of Elisha the prophet; and none of them was cleansed, but only Naaman the Syrian." And all in the synagogue were filled with rage as they heard these things; and they rose up and cast Him out of the city, and led Him to the brow of the hill on which their city had been built, in order to throw Him down the cliff. But passing through their midst, He went His way.*

The Story Detailed

The Return to Nazareth

Following the temptation episodes Jesus turned toward Galilee, settling in Capernaum, fulfilling the prophecy from Isaiah 9:1 (Matthew 4:12-16). Capernaum served as sort of a home base for Jesus during much of His ministry years. Nazareth is about twenty miles south and west from Capernum. Capernaum had a population of approximately two to four thousand people when Jesus set up His headquarters there. Nazareth had approximately fifty or so people. It was from here that Jesus began His ministry of preaching and teaching that the "kingdom of heaven is near" (Matthew 4:17).

Both Matthew and Mark record that Jesus set out from Capernaum to go to Nazareth. Matthew records that Jesus visited His hometown about two years into His ministry after He finished the kingdom parables by the sea. There were many intervening events between the parables and this visit to Nazareth -- some which include:

- Calming the storm on the sea (Matthew 8:23-27)
- Healing the Gadarene demoniac (Matthew 8:28-34)
- Healing Jairus' daughter (Matthew 9:18, 19, 23-26)
- Healing the hemorrhaging woman as she touched Him (Matthew 9:20-22)

Interestingly, Matthew recorded the events of Jesus' visit to Nazareth but did not record the sermon He preached. This is unusual for him since he recorded the messages of Jesus more than any other evangelist. It is also interesting to note that after the event in Nazareth, the disciples were sent out two by two for the first time (Mark 6:7).

It was typical of Him to leave and come back to Capernaum throughout those first two years. This time, however, Jesus left Capernaum permanently. He was the traveling evangelist who moved on at the impulse of the Spirit, and the Spirit plainly indicated that there would be no more fruit to be picked in this northern region. D.L. Moody used to operate the same way, his diary tells us. He would schedule meetings in a town and would announce no closing date. This he left up to the Spirit of God. His diary records that when the team sensed that the Spirit was not present for bringing sinners under conviction, then the whole team left no matter how many days they had been there.

On His way out of the Galilean region, Jesus stopped at Nazareth. It was a courtesy call on the town that had been His home for twenty-six or twenty-seven years. His visit could have been in response to the requests of His mother and brothers (Matthew 12:46-50), or it could also have been because of some tragedy in the family or a lack of funds to support the remaining brothers and sisters. What is interesting about Jesus' ministry beginning at thirty years of age is that this would have probably given all the brothers and sisters the opportunity to grow up and be on their own. There is some suggestion that His mother began following Him during this visit.

Jesus, coming to the town of His family, would no doubt be expected to stay at the family home. Even though His disciples (more than the Twelve) were with Him, He would be expected to make His family home His operating center. This is what probably prompted the comment that one gets no honor in one's own household. Imagine the scene: Jesus is back home, rooming in the house where He is just the son of a carpenter. His unbelieving brothers are coming in and out of those familiar hallways and rooms. His disciples, who are completely committed to His being the Messiah, must surely make a stark contrast with the insolent and disrespectful brothers. Their lack of belief added fuel on the fire of the town's unbelief: "Look, if even His own family doesn't see anything special about Him, why should we?"

The implication from Mark's passage is that Jesus arrived a few days before the Sabbath, which would only heighten this incredible paradox between His blood family and His new family of believers. This paradox is often the case for the Christian where his or her family is skeptical and rude about one's belief, faith, and life, while those who share a common faith are one's real family even though they aren't blood relatives. Jesus was really a radical in this area for He suggested that one's faith is stronger than blood ties (Matthew 12:46-50). It is encouraging to note that Jesus had to juggle this double commitment even though He laid greater priority upon the family of faith. Many a holiday has been ruined because it is spent with the blood family out of obligation, rather than with the family of faith in celebration.

Teaching at the Synagogue

The culmination of every week was the Sabbath. On that particular Sabbath, a hometown boy of increasing fame throughout the land was to be a special guest preacher. Jesus was an eloquent speaker and a powerful worker of miracles.

Everyone had heard what He had been doing twenty miles north in Capernaum, and the episode at Cana of Galilee just four miles away was still strong in their memory. Mark records that there were many listeners. Certainly no one wanted to miss Jesus, the famous hometown boy.

Their anticipation must have been electric as they waited for Him to do great things. Why, if He had done incredible things in Capernaum and Cana, then just imagine what He would do in His own hometown! There's no telling what their miracle worker would do.

Jesus continued doing what He always did on the Sabbath -- He went to the synagogue to teach and do much work. The open policy of synagogues provided a platform on which to teach, and the fact that it was the Sabbath exposed His teaching to the maximum amount of people. It also allowed people to follow Jesus on their day off, unencumbered with the things of the world (they were already in a religious mode). Jesus was incredibly smart to tailor His unique ministry around the cultural framework of the people. He taught on the day they expected to be taught and on the day they were already directed toward God. Even though Jesus used this cultural framework, He did not mandate it upon His disciples (Romans 14:6).

The open policy of the synagogue was that any preacher could preach a message to the assembly if He had permission from the ruler or rulers of the synagogue. This was not difficult for Jesus to obtain in His hometown now that He had become famous. This would, however, explain why Jesus had to move on when the religious leaders of the city became hardened against Him. They had the power to effectively shut

Him out of the synagogue's pulpits. The time at the synagogue would have looked something like this:

- Blessings or thanksgivings (usually chanted)
- Prayer with response of "Amen" by the congregation
- Reading of a passage from the Pentateuch (in Hebrew followed by translation in Aramaic)
- Reading of a passage from the Prophets (in Hebrew followed by translation in Aramaic)
- Sermon or word of exhortation
- Benediction pronounced by a priest to which the congregation responded with "Amen." When no priest was present, a closing prayer was substituted for the benediction.

Luke gives us a much more complete picture of what took place inside the synagogue of Nazareth on that fateful day. He details Jesus' part in the synagogue service, the sermon, as well as the events that took place outside after the service.

Following the reading of twenty-seven verses of the Pentateuch -- three verses by seven readers -- Jesus stood up to read the prophetic portion for the service. He is handed the scroll of Isaiah. He probably asked for this particular scroll to be given to Him so that the text and the sermon would be unified.

Jesus opened the scroll and found Isaiah 61:1,2. It is suggested that this is just the reading for the day, placing this Sabbath on the Day of Atonement. This idea, however, seems to lack support from early Hebrew lexicons and from the positive statement that Jesus Himself sought out that particular text.

He quoted Isaiah 61:1,2a and stopped before the section on "the day of vengeance of our God." This is significant because Jesus knew at this point that His mission would be a two-part mission and that the Jews were not going to accept Him as Messiah (Matthew 12). God was not ready to wreak vengeance upon the world until the Savior's work and glory could be spread around the globe. It was God's mercy that did not allow Jesus to read the rest of verse 2 which He had started. Jesus knew His mission. He was to only accomplish this certain amount at this time. The problem with Christians is that they are either lagging behind God and His work schedule, or they are trying to get ahead of God and do too much too early. *"Those who wait on the Lord shall renew their strength."*

Luke put this episode at the beginning of the narrative on the Galilean ministry to highlight the rejection He would suffer eventually in every place but also to put the anointing of the Spirit at Jesus' baptism near Jesus' declaration that the Spirit of the Lord did indeed reside upon Him. It is the Spirit of the Lord that allowed Jesus to accomplish the mission for which He had been sent.

Luke's gospel details the verses that Jesus read prior to His sermon. Luke 4:17-19 says this:

> *And the book of the prophet Isaiah was handed to Him. And He opened the book and found the place where it was written, "The Spirit of the Lord is upon me, because He anointed me to preach the gospel to the poor. He has sent me to proclaim release to the*

captives, and recovery of sight to the blind, to set free those who are oppressed, to proclaim the favorable year of the Lord."

These verses were either those directly related to Jesus' sermon, or they were very unusual as the reading of the Prophets usually included twenty-seven verses. Readings could also be as little as three verses if commentary on each were included but never only two verses. It seems best to conclude that this is exactly the way Jesus read the verses and that the shock value of the short passage was intended to gain attention.

Each concept in these verses is crucial for it explains a part of the ministry of Jesus and why the Jews had such a difficult time with His goals. Jesus' ideas work on two levels and give a fascinating explanation of the way He thinks.

1. Preach the gospel to the poor

The poor were an oppressed lot and the Messiah was to give them good news. The Jews, however, had concluded that the only good news you can give a poor person is the ways or means to obtain wealth. There seemed to be the underlying belief that the Messiah would institute some new order to eliminate poverty. Jesus never moved in the direction of suggesting that the good news He came to proclaim to the poor was how to become wealthy or that He would institute land reform or redistribute wealth. We do know that He did contribute to the poor out of the ministry coffers, but this did not seem to be a major theme.

The Jews believed that if one was rich, God was sending a signal that you were a blessed person. They also believed that to be poor was a signal that you resided under the judgment of God. It is not a very far jump to begin believing that only rich people can be saved. Jesus declared that He would preach the good news to the poor, meaning that your monetary worth has nothing to do with your standing before God. Jesus said that the way to God is open to everyone. It comes through poverty of spirit. Without internal reform and spiritual poverty, all economic reform is only a quick fix. The best news comes to those who are poor -- poor in spirit. It is this kind of people who will inherit the kingdom of heaven (Matthew 5:3). Humility, teachability, and submission – these qualities are crucial to a relationship with God.

2. Proclaim release to the captives

The underlying image of this verse is one of a conquered people under the bondage of a foreign nation suffering through the chains of slavery and the sting of the whip. The Jews thought that the Messiah would not only institute some economic reform but also remove the oppression of Rome. It was this hope of getting out from under the tyranny of Rome that excited the Jews. But Jesus did not in any way suggest that He would free the captives in this way. In fact, He directed an even greater submission through His second-mile lifestyle. Jesus saw an even greater oppression and slavery. The people were enslaved to sin and Satan. Governments can only hold the body, but these other two can hold the very heart of man. Jesus said in John 8:34 that the super-religious Jews were slaves to sin. This was followed by the declaration that they were in the family and service of Satan, the Great Evil One. Jesus did not come to remove governmental oppression but a greater oppression. His death and resurrection canceled the power of our enslavement, but too often the former prisoners stay in their cells because it is familiar and comfortable.

Jesus Visits His Hometown

3. Recovery of sight to the blind

This is really an amazing picture. In Isaiah 61, this verse is translated as "freedom to the prisoners" but by Jesus as "sight to the blind." The image is one of a prisoner in the dark dungeon of captivity being released and all of a sudden light falling on the eyes that had been useless before (i.e., blind). Jesus did heal many who were blind and gave them the gift of physical sight, but He left some blind still without sight. If His mission had been strictly physical, then He failed in His mission. Therefore it is clear that this reference is to a spiritual blindness.

The *prison* in which men are enslaved is operated by sin and Satan, meaning that the blind eyes need the light of Christ to expose the enslavement. Even though the prisoners' eyes functioned before, they were virtually useless because of the lack of light. Our understanding may be functioning but is useless until we have the information and truth supplied by Christ to give us an adequate picture of what is really happening in the world -- that those without Jesus Christ as their light are blind to their imprisonment.

4. To set free those who are oppressed (or downtrodden)

Jesus sought to have the people understand that oppression was so much more than the governmental oppression they were suffering under Rome. They were under a soul-crushing oppression. What they could be and what they could do for God had been stolen from them. They were at the mercy of much greater enemies: the world, sin, and Satan. These had them under their thumbs. Jesus proclaimed release -- the "Good News!" -- that we don't have to follow the lusts of the flesh and the direction of the deceiver. Unfortunately, so few have accepted the offer of the tremendous freedom that is possible in Christ Jesus. If we are going to let Jesus do His ministry in our hearts, we must be willing to let Him change the way we think. He wants us to pursue a different life than what we were pursuing under the oppression of the past. There is so much more that God has built us to accomplish than the narrow, dysfunctional path that our world, our selfishness, and the Devil want us to live. Break free in life by allowing Jesus to show you new ways of living. Let Him give you new goals that can bless others and change your world.

5. To proclaim the favorable Year of the Lord
The reference here is to the Year of Jubilee. Every fifty years God had mandated a year in which there was to be no sowing or reaping of the land but instead it was to be given a rest. It was also a time of letting the slaves go free and a chance for the land to revert back to its original owner. By the time Jesus reads these words, the Jews had been in the land over a thousand years and they never once celebrated one of these jubilee years. God, through Jesus, says that He would institute the Year of Jubilee and fulfill its provisions in the land. Jesus was God's provision for the fulfillment. He would do a renovation of the heart that would release people from their clinging and greedy ways.

It was their mistake to not make adequate inner preparation to be ready for the ultimate fulfillment. They had been hoping this day would come, but they had not thought how different their lives would be if it actually came. When they began grappling with the implications, they rejected the liberator because His program would result in too much change.

In the middle of the verse Jesus abruptly stopped and closed the scroll. Not only did He not read enough verses, but He also stopped in the middle of a verse -- one that the Jews uniquely loved. The next phrase says, "The day of vengeance of our God." This meant that God would finally take vengeance on those who afflicted Israel. To stop in the middle of this prophecy was sure to catch everyone's attention and further cause some to scream "Blasphemy!" for they had no forgiveness for their oppressors; they wanted none of the mercy, love, and forgiveness that Jesus was preaching. The hate that filled their hearts spilled over into their relationship with Jesus as we shall see. The Jews had built a neat container for their hate. They practiced loving their neighbor, but they openly proclaimed that it was okay to hate your enemy. Because of this the Jews held the Romans in utter contempt and saw no problem with hating the Romans while loving fellow Jews. It is always a mistake to believe that you can corral hate in one quadrant of your life. If you allow it in any part of your life, it ends up corrupting the whole.

Jesus gave the scroll back to the attendant and sat down; a signal that He wanted to preach. One stood to read Scripture out of respect for the Word of God but sat down to preach in order that one's energy might go into the power of His words. The eyes of the crowd were riveted upon Jesus. All the various techniques He used to gain attention worked. He made sure that He had their attention, knowing it was useless to preach or teach if He did not have the attention of the audience.

We do not have the whole of the sermon that Jesus preached on this occasion, but we do have the point: "The verses I have read have been fulfilled today." This was even more shocking than what Jesus had done to gain attention. This type of idea would have immediately solicited the question in the hearers' minds: "Who do you want us to think you are?" Jesus was revealing Himself to them as the Messiah, asking them to make a commitment to Him. He wanted the benefits of Isaiah 61:1,2 to take place in their lives. Remember, this was His hometown where He grew up. Jesus never shied away from the issues or reduced the level of the commitment. Unfortunately, the commitment He was asking them to make proved to be a great hurdle for the folks who had seen Him grow up.

Jesus employed a teaching technique that demanded the sermon be finished in the minds of the hearers. He didn't windup a sermon in a nice neat package but rather left the hearer hanging, asking questions, and discussing implications inside their heads. It is in this way that Jesus' teaching reaches a depth that never fails to motivate.

The Response of the People

Immediately after the sermon, the service was over. The crowds that had gathered began to marvel at how wonderful their favorite son had done. He had preached extremely well. He had kept their attention riveted to Scripture. What wisdom! They were absolutely amazed at how wise and commanding His sermon had been. Following the service at the synagogue, Mark's gospel records this:

> Mark 6:2-3 - *He began to teach in the synagogue: and the many listeners were astonished, saying, "Where did this man get these things, and what is this wisdom given to Him, and such miracles as these performed by His hands? Is not this the carpenter, the son of Mary, and brother of James, and Joseph, and Judas, and Simon? Are not His sisters here with us?" And they took offense at Him.*

Jesus Visits His Hometown

The verses note that the people were astonished about three things concerning Jesus: "these things," "this wisdom," and "such miracles." Let's take a closer look at their reaction:

1. "These things" probably referred to His ability to command attention and teach with power and authority. He was the master teacher! It must have been something to sit at the feet of the best teacher to ever walk the planet and listen to Him as He moved your mind just where He wanted it to go. Yes, there are ways that a message can be presented that makes it easier to listen. Jesus used many of these techniques.

2. "This wisdom" most likely referred to Jesus' ability to interpret Scripture and make it incredibly practical, plus He was able to bring out hidden wisdom in a passage they had heard for years. He really made the Scriptures come alive. Just when they had thought they had heard every idea and application on every passage, Jesus shared insights and practical application they had never heard before. He brought freshness and life back to the Word of God. Of course one would expect this from the living Word of God, right? There is a tendency in churches today to want to hear something new from the Scriptures but to not do anything with it. Wisdom refuses to be ignored. If you hear it, it makes you do something with its points.

3. "Such miracles" couldn't refer to the miracles that He did in Nazareth because their unbelief kept Him from doing any there (Matthew 13:58). It is likely that this

referred to the reports about His miracle-working powers that had filtered into Nazareth from Capernaum and the surrounding region. Surely they were well acquainted with the stories about this miracle-working prophet. They did not doubt the accuracy of the stories.

All of these were irrefutable things that could not be denied or easily dismissed. The evidence was strong that this man was special and was telling them the truth. However, they could not escape the conclusion of His message that kept coming back to them. If He was right about what He said, then He (Jesus) is the Messiah. If He was right about what this Scripture meant, then they would have to put their full faith in Him.

So what stopped them from believing? Matthew tells us that they examined His family background and came to the conclusion that there was no reasonable explanation as to why He should be believed. In essence, they questioned His pedigree! This brought up a mental faith hurdle for them because they knew this man. They had watched Him grow up. Had He not played with their children? Was He not the son of the carpenter, Joseph? The mental hurdle continued to expand as they realized the wonderful and amazing nature of His words and works. They couldn't deny that Jesus said things wise beyond what they had ever heard before or that He had performed many miracles nearby. But they could not find a logical reason for them, and they refused to believe in Him. This is like so many today that reject the grace, mercy, and power of God because they are unable to explain how it works. But unlike people today, these people were actually there!

Ultimately their unbelief came down to one thing: They could not explain why the blessings had fallen on this lowly carpenter's son. They were aware of His upbringing and the fact that He had attended no special schools. He had no degrees and had not tutored at the feet of a great rabbi. This was very important to them back then, and it seems to be that way even today. It is a sad day when one is listened to depending on where they went to school or with whom they studied. But the tutelage of the Holy Spirit is sufficient for a teacher of the truth. The Scriptures themselves are a guidebook and will yield the correct doctrines if one studies carefully. The Bible says that God will guide you into all truth. God the Father and God the Spirit were Jesus' teachers; and they, along with Christ, can be ours as well if we are willing to give our time and concentration.

I believe the people of Nazareth weren't able to receive Jesus' message because they weren't prepared to hear it. Sadly, this town of Nazareth was only twenty miles from the headquarters of Jesus' ministry for the last two years and yet there is no evidence that these people ever made the journey. Some may have walked the twenty miles, but there was so much unbelief in Nazareth. They were too caught up in the day-to-day affairs of life to stop and search for God's new man to the Jewish nation. There is a great danger in getting so wrapped up in life that we never stop and pursue God. Their lack of a searching heart betrayed them when the man they should have sought out came to them. It is not true that you can put off searching for God until later when it is more convenient. For those people it was never more convenient than it was that day, and yet they did not respond in faith.

The issue of faith in the city of Nazareth is true for all of us. We can only move forward in our spiritual life through faith. God is not going to work in your life unless you can believe Him and move forward in trust. Is God asking you to have faith to move in some direction, but you are having a hard time expressing faith for some secondary reason? There are numerous areas where God may be asking you to trust His way of living: marriage, family, money, friends, personal development, and spirituality. Ask God if you are failing to trust Him in any of these areas as the people of Nazareth did.

Jesus' Response

So how did Jesus respond to the rejection He experienced by those who knew Him personally? Luke 4:23 records that He quoted a proverb, letting them know He was aware of what they were thinking: "Physician, heal yourself! Whatever we heard was done at Capernaum, do here in your hometown as well." He seemed to specifically needle the group into taking action to make them understand who He really was. This was a proverb of derision. If He were so great, then surely He would do as much -- if not more -- at home than on the road. They may have also been pointing out that His own family didn't seem to be enjoying the blessings of His so-called ministry. Wasn't His mother still under the boot of Rome and the whole family still poor? Jesus' Spirit-directed ability to understand the thoughts and intents of people's hearts opened the oozing bitterness of their resentment against Him for doing nothing for their little town.

Jesus' rejection here is very similar to the rejection by the Pharisees in Matthew 12. The Pharisees chose not to believe in Him and then demanded a sign from Him so that they might believe. In this case, they turned away because of the mental hurdles of His family status and His lack of formal education. He let them know that He was aware they wanted a sign, but He is not in the magic show business. He does not perform on-demand miracles to prove things to a skeptical audience. He unleashes the power of God when and only when God the Father directs.

This taunt that came from the mind of the Nazarites was very similar to the jeers that were hurled at Him upon the cross: "He saved others, but He cannot save Himself?" To answer their question, Jesus responded to their subconscious proverb with another proverb: "No prophet is without honor except in his hometown" (Luke 4:24). In Mark's gospel He added three other groups to those who rejected His claims at that time: His own hometown, relatives, and household (Mark 6:4). Let's examine each of these groups that withheld honor from those to whom it was due:

1. A prophet's hometown

This obviously refers to Jesus' hometown of Nazareth and their lack of belief and pride in God's sovereign choosing of one of their own. We discussed this in the previous section in more detail. Essentially they were jealous that someone of Jesus' caliber (or lack of it) could experience the great blessings of God. Remember that to the Jews of that time wealth and education were seen as evidence of God's favor. In other words if you did not have wealth or status, God could not be blessing you. In our day and age we think this way about fame, position, power, and money. If a person does not have these things, then how could God be blessing them? So Jesus' life of divine blessing turned their thinking upside down. We, too, are called to live a life of quiet godliness and loving God and others with Christ's power. A life full of loving relationship and righteousness that comes from God rebukes the values of the world.

2. A prophet's own relatives

Jesus must have suffered the sting of rejection from His relatives. The whole countryside was probably filled with the relations of Mary and Joseph. To them, Jesus was that "different" child -- the one who forced Joseph to marry the "loose" woman. Who even knows about His father? It is probable that many of the relatives would have shunned this family because of the questionable nature of Jesus' birth, and also because Mary was probably a young widow desirable to other husbands. Remember that widows were also thought of as somehow cursed by God (for why else would God have taken their husbands?). Mary's whole life seemed like a tragedy, and she had made a tragedy of Joseph's life also. The whole ugly business seemed to center around this different firstborn son, Jesus. And hadn't he run off and left His family to pursue some itinerant preaching ministry? Jesus knew the sting of rejection from relatives.

When we feel the sting of rejection by our family for following Jesus, He can relate to us as He suffered the same fate. There are always family members who twist our story around and destroy us with it. We must accept that when we follow God and do His will for our lives, not everyone will jump up and down and get excited about what we are doing. It was not this way with Jesus, and it will not necessarily be this way with us.

3. A prophet's own household

There was no glory coming from His immediate family

either. There was just gossip, rumor, and slander. They were skeptical to say the least. None of them believed in Him until after the resurrection. A dispute with His brothers is recorded in John's gospel (John 7:1-8) about going up to the festival. Paraphrasing, they challenged Jesus saying, "If you really desired to be a big-time prophet, then get with it and show yourself in Jerusalem!" The man, Jesus, was truly humble, a man of sorrows, and acquainted with grief.

If you've heard the concept that "familiarity breeds contempt," this is a prime example. Those who should have been His biggest boosters were the most skeptical. How tragic! It is very instructive that His brothers, James and Jude, became believers in Him and led parts of the church after the resurrection. Tradition tells us that James was even martyred for his faith! This is strong testimony from a skeptic. His family did turn around and were able to weave all the various threads of their memory into solid evidence for His Messiahship.

Matthew and Mark do not record the entirety of the incident that caused the townspeople to become upset. But Jesus continued His provocative style by letting the people know, in a most unflattering way, that only those who had faith would receive God's benefit; and they did not have such faith. He called them out for their lack of faith by telling them stories of foreigners who had faith in God while God's people didn't believe.

Luke records that Jesus told two stories from the Old Testament to explain why they (the townspeople of Nazareth) were excluded from the blessing of His miracles. First, He tells the story of the widow of Zarephath to whom God sent

Elijah during the famine in Israel. There were many widows in need in Israel, but God sent His miracle worker to a Phoenician widow because she had a need and she exercised faith. She believed that what was proclaimed in the name of the Jehovah God about her flour and oil not running dry would come true. How sad that in all Israel there were no safe and faithful places to send Elijah. The people of God became deserters and idolaters that did not fear God. Jesus is telling these Jews, who saw themselves as pious, that they were being rejected because of their lack of faith in what God could do.

Jesus strengthens the point by telling of Elijah's successor, Elisha, and about how there were many lepers in the land of Israel but only a hated pagan Syrian General had the faith to come and pursue healing by the Lord God of Israel. The account tells us he was healed after believing the Word of God through Elisha. Naaman was instructed to wash in the Jordan seven times. He initially rejected this faith exercise but eventually did what Elisha suggested as a matter of faith and was healed of leprosy. How tragic that only a foreigner who had not grown up surrounded by the law and miracles of God would put more faith in Jehovah than the chosen people of God! Yet another example of how familiarity breeds contempt.

The crowd that gathered outside the synagogue to discuss the sermon clearly got the point. Luke 4:28 records that they were filled with rage as they heard these things. They were incensed that Jesus would imply that the pagan Gentiles of Capernaum were more worthy of God's blessings than the strict, devout Jews of His own hometown. How dare He suggest that they were not righteous and that they didn't have faith! He compared them to the unrighteous idolaters who caused Israel to be taken captive. Unbelievable!

Jesus' point was that miracles come to those who are ready to put faith into action by relying on the revealed Word of God. These people were not ready. They were too caught up in why God gave these blessings to this man and what schooling and education Jesus went through to speak these wonderful things. They did not doubt that all of Jesus' gifts were from God. They refused to put their understanding into action by believing on Jesus to be the One to provide the means of God's blessings. Don't let your mental hang-ups with the channel of God's love and blessing keep you from receiving the blessings. Unfortunately many people believe all the right things but allow certain mental hurdles to keep them from putting their "knowledge" into action.

The people became so offended with what He said that they put their hate into action and pushed Jesus to the head of an angry mob. Their intent was to push Him off a cliff on the edge of town. They wanted to kill Him. Don't you wonder whether Jesus kept talking and said, "The type of action you are engaged in right now is the type you should use with your faith"? They were acting, but it was giving vent to the wrong impulse.

Alfred Edershiem, in his book, *The Life and Times of Jesus the Messiah,* suggests that on the southwest corner of the town there is a cliff which is the only one large enough to kill a person if he were pushed off.[1] The townspeople herded Jesus toward this spot in absolute rage -- probably yelling, shouting, and gnashing their teeth. At some point along the angry journey Jesus slipped from their midst. God the Father and

God the Spirit had provided Jesus with a way of escape. He would die at the hands of an angry mob but not here and not now. God will always give us ways of escape to thwart the plans of the Devil and/or evil men unless he wants to use their anger for his grand plan.

How did He escape? Perhaps the blindness of the angry mob rendered His escape possible if Jesus had slowed down in the middle of the mob and let the leaders proceed on without Him. Also, His disciples who surely came along might have followed along and provided some friendly faces to distract them. However it happened, the power of the Spirit of God would surely have been operating to give Him the chance to slip away unnoticed. Imagine the peoples' surprise having made it to the edge of the cliff only to find that Jesus was no longer in their midst. It is important to recognize that Jesus left early and did not expect God to wait until after He was plunging to the bottom of the ravine to rescue Him. This would have proved nothing. God had provided a way of escape early in the process to what was a sure conclusion. Make sure you are wise and look for an escape hatch early in the process. Do not be foolish and allow yourself to be tempted into believing that God must provide a way of escape right at the very end (1 Corinthians 10:13). Many times we unknowingly pass up God's best escape routes.

The Apostle Paul tells us of eight basic weapons for spiritual warfare. He calls them the Armor of God. They are spiritual weapons to be used when we are battling spiritual opposition and spiritual enemies. In this case Jesus uses the fifth weapon called *salvation*. The word is *sozo* in the Greek which means a way of escape. Jesus is our ultimate way of escape from the spiritual war we are facing. But God will provide various

Jesus Visits His Hometown

ways of escape during the course of our lives to allow us to defeat Satan.

On their way out of town, Matthew and Mark record that Jesus was amazed at the unbelief in His hometown. Just as they had wondered at His wisdom, He wondered at their incredible unbelief. It was incredible because they believed in everything He did; they would just not believe in Him as their Messiah. They refused to come to Him for saving help.

Mark states that Jesus did not do many miracles there because of the people's unbelief. It was not that Jesus was without power to do miracles because they did not believe in Him; rather, it was that no one came to have miracles performed upon them. Incredible, but the greatest prophet and miracle worker was making His triumphant return home and there were not enough people coming to Him to keep Him busy. It would be like J. Paul Getty returning to his hometown to stand on the street corner to hand out $100 bills and only passing out a few because people did not want to accept money from Him. Another point concerning the lack of miracles in this town was that doing miracles to an unreceptive audience does not produce believers, but skeptics, as Jesus' miracles performed before the Pharisees demonstrated.

The blessings of God are all around, ready to be claimed by those willing to seek for them. They hang like ripe fruit from the vines of the Word of God. They are arranged like gold nuggets in the will of God, but very few are those who will travel that way. And even fewer will stoop down in humility and receive the precious blessings God gives. It was tragic for the people of Nazareth to reject all the help they would ever need for any problem. It is just as tragic for us to neglect the promises of the Word of God and the joys of knowing Christ. Don't let some cultural, mental, emotional, or any other reason keep you from putting your full faith in Jesus Christ and His will for your life. Remember, "I can do all things through Christ who strengthens me."

Delighting in Jesus

This chapter is about Jesus announcing what He came to do for individuals and the need for faith. It is important to take time to remember what He has done in these three areas: healing our spiritual blindness; overcoming spiritual, mental, and even physical oppression in our lives; and providing ways of escape to get around the evil aimed at us. Take a look at each of these three areas and delight in all that Jesus has done and is doing. Also take a look at where Jesus wants you to trust Him.

Expressing faith in Him to work in your life
God wants to do impossible things in your life, and He wants to head you in a different direction than where your selfishness takes you. To do that, He needs you to trust Him. Is there an area where God is asking you to trust Him and yet you are having a hard time doing that because of your past, something you heard, or some fear? Check out the issue and then trust God and move forward.

Spiritual blindness

Delight in the fact that Jesus has come to set you free from the spiritual blindness that you have known and from the oppression that sin, the world, and Satan are pushing on you. As I look at my life, I can see areas of spiritual blindness that Christ has touched. Can you point to areas of truth, relationships, or situations that Jesus has healed in your life?

Spiritual, mental, and physical oppression

I can also see how Satan tries to confine my ways of thinking about my parents, my vocation, my friends, and myself. The Devil was trying to get me to act out of my wrong thinking to destroy these relationships and my potential. There is so much more that you can accomplish in life when you allow Jesus to show you a new way of thinking and acting. What is Jesus trying to show you right now? What are new areas to open up His power and love?

Ways of escape

In the midst of life, the Devil will attempt to trap us through a number of difficulties and problems. God will give us ways of escape or "salvations" so we will not have to give into temptation, difficulties, or problems. But we must be ready for them when they come. Just as Jesus slipped through the crowd because He knew it was not His time, we can be alert to when God will give us a way out of a relationship, a job, or some situation. Is God giving you a way out of a dangerous, tempting, or overwhelming situation? Take His way of escape.

Chapter 4
The Feeding of the Five Thousand

Key Verses

Matthew 14:13-23 - *Now when Jesus heard it, He withdrew from there in a boat, to a lonely place by Himself; and when the multitudes heard of this, they followed Him on foot from the cities. And when He went ashore, He saw a great multitude, He felt compassion for them, and healed their sick. And when it was evening, the disciples came to Him, saying, "The place is desolate, and the time is already past; send the multitudes away, that they may go into the villages and buy food for themselves." But Jesus said to them, "They do not need to go away; you give them something to eat!" And they said to Him, "We have here only five loaves and two fish." And He said, "Bring them here to Me." And ordering the multitudes to recline on the grass, He took the five loaves and the two fish, and looking up toward heaven, He blessed the food, and breaking the loaves He gave them to the disciples, and the disciples gave to the multitudes, and they all ate, and were satisfied. And they picked up what was left over of the broken pieces, twelve full baskets. And there were about five thousand men who ate, aside from women and children. And immediately He made the disciples get into the boat, and go ahead of Him to the other side, while He sent the multitudes away. And after He had sent the multitudes away, He went up to the mountain by Himself to pray; and when it was evening, He was there alone.*

Mark 6:33-44 - *And the people saw them going, and many recognized them, and they ran there together on foot from all the cities, and got there ahead of them. And when He went ashore, He saw a great multitude, and He felt compassion for them because they were like sheep without a shepherd; and He began to teach them many things. And when it was already quite late, His disciples came up to Him and began saying, "The place is desolate and it is already quite late; send them away so that they may go into the surrounding countryside and villages and buy themselves something to eat." But He answered and said to them, "You give them something to eat!" And they said to Him, "Shall we go and spend two hundred denarii on bread and give them something to eat?" And He said to them, "How many loaves do you have? Go look!" And when they found out, they said, "Five and two fish." And He commanded them all to recline by groups on the green grass. And they reclined in companies of hundreds and of fifties. And He took the five loaves and the two fish, and looking up toward heaven, He blessed the food and broke the loaves and He kept giving them to the disciples to set before them, and He divided up the two fish among them all. And they all ate and were satisfied. And they picked up twelve full baskets of the broken pieces, and also of the fish. And there were five thousand men who ate the loaves.*

Luke 9:10-17 - *And when the apostles returned, they gave an account to Him of all that they had done. And taking them with Him, He withdrew by Himself to a city called Bethsaida. But the multitudes were aware of this and followed Him; and welcoming them, He began speaking to them about the kingdom of God and curing those who had need of healing. And the day began to decline, and the twelve came and said to Him, "Send the multitude away, that they may go into the surrounding villages and countryside and find lodging and get something to eat; for here we are in a desolate place." But He said to them, "You give them something to eat!" And*

The Feeding of the Five Thousand

they said, "We have no more than five loaves and two fish, unless perhaps we go and buy food for all these people." (For there were about five thousand men.) And He said to His disciples, "Have them recline to eat in groups of about fifty each." And they did so, and had them all recline. And He took the five loaves and the two fish, and looking up to heaven, He blessed them, and broke them, and kept giving them to the disciples to set before the multitude. And they all ate and were satisfied; and the broken pieces which they had left over were picked up, twelve baskets full.

John 6:1-14 - *After these things Jesus went away to the other aide of the Sea of Galilee (or Tiberias). And a great multitude was following Him, because they were seeing the signs He was performing on those who were sick. And Jesus went up on the mountain, and there He sat with His disciples. Now the Passover, the feast of the Jews, was at hand. Jesus therefore lifted up His eyes, and seeing that a great multitude was coming to Him, said to Philip, "Where are we to buy bread, that these may eat?" And this He was saying to test Him; for He Himself knew what He was intending to do. Philip answered Him "Two hundred denarii worth of bread is not sufficient for them, for everyone to receive a little." One of His disciples, Andrew, Simon Peter's brother, said to Him, "There is a lad here who has five barley loaves and two fish, but what are these for so many people?" Jesus said, "Have the people sit down." Now there was much grass in the place. So the men sat down, in number about five thousand. Jesus therefore took the loaves; and having given thanks, He distributed to those who were seated; likewise also of the fish as much as they wanted. And when they were filled, He said to His disciples, "Gather up the leftover fragments that nothing may be lost." And so they gathered them up, and filled twelve baskets with fragments from the five barley loaves, which were left over by those who had eaten. When therefore the people saw the sign which He had performed, they said, "This is truly the Prophet who is to come into the world."*

The Story Detailed

The Setting

Jesus was in Capernaum having just returned from a preaching tour that had taken Him to the cities where the disciples preached and healed. This had been the disciples' first preaching excursion having been sent out two by two into various cities to tell the people to "Repent -- the kingdom of God is at hand!" Mark 6:7-13 tells us that Jesus also gave them authority to cast out demons, anoint the sick, and heal many people. This expansion of the preachers could help account for the extra large crowd that was following them that day.

After the disciples had given their account of all that had happened on the trip, the text tells us that they withdrew with Jesus by boat. There are three reasons for this.

1. He knew the disciples needed rest

The text is adamant about the need for rest as it states that the apostles -- who now could heal diseases, cast out demons, raise the dead, and preach -- were deluged like Jesus was with requests for service. They were constantly in demand and so busy that they needed to eat in shifts. A few of them were no doubt outside the house taking care of the requests while the others were inside eating. Imagine the crush of people and the variety of needs. Undoubtedly they were exhausted and overwhelmed. The price of success was beginning to take its toll on the whole group.

In a move to ensure some peace, Jesus herded the Twelve onto a boat at the seashore of Capernaum. They set sail for

The Feeding of the Five Thousand

Bethsaida in Phillip the Tetrarch's district. With the sail hoisted and the direction set, the quiet and gentle lapping of the waves must have been a welcome relief from the constant clamor of the crowds. Jesus seemed to understand that He owed this multitude nothing in comparison to what He owed His disciples. He was not tempted by the crowd to stay around to do one more miracle.

It is fascinating that the rest Jesus was interested in never took place unless one considers a few hours in the boat and the opportunity to sit down on a hill as a retreat. We know this because the very same day they sailed back in the direction of Capernaum. It was in Capernaum the next day that Jesus preached the famous "I am the Bread of Life" sermon. Following that day, Jesus and the disciples had plenty of time to rest for many of the disciples no longer walked with Him because of the difficulty of His sayings. Jesus was becoming popular and multitudes were following Him for all the wrong reasons. He needed to thin the herd.

2. He needed to escape Herod's reach following John the Baptist's murder

We are not told how the groups of disciples were divided up or who arrived back to Capernaum first, but they were all present when news about the murder of John the Baptist reached Jesus' ears. John's murder took place on Herod Antipas's birthday. Salome, his adulteress wife's daughter, danced for Him and was promised anything including up to half of Herod's kingdom. She asked her mother what to ask for and she replied, "Ask for the head of John the Baptist." Her reason was that Herod loved listening to him, and John spoke out boldly about how wrong it was for Herod to have stolen his brother's wife.

Herod Antipas had heard about the miracles that Jesus had been doing and somehow in his twisted mind became convinced that Jesus was the resurrected form of John the Baptist. Capernaum was in Herod's jurisdiction, so Jesus saw the need to cool down Herod's desire to find Him by going outside of the boundaries of Herod's territory. Herod Antipas's brother, Phillip, was tetrarch of the region into which Jesus withdrew. He knew He could reasonably expect to find shelter from Herod in Phillip's district because of the animosity between the brothers.

3. There was a popular sentiment to make Christ king

Alfred Edershiem, in his book, *The Life and Times of Jesus the Messiah,* suggests another reason for the departure of Jesus from Capernaum. John's murder would have increased popular discontent with Herod and so the people might have sought to make Jesus their king by force. This revolt was something Jesus consistently avoided as He had no use for earthly power.[1] The Jews of that time were looking for the spark that would ignite national revolt against the Romans. The Scripture records a number of "would be" military messiahs.

This episode in the life and ministry of Jesus took place in the spring of Jesus' second year, possibly April of 29 A.D. One year later at the Passover, Jesus was crucified by an angry mob's words, "Crucify Him! Crucify Him!"

The Destination

Bethsaida was their destination. It was one of two Bethsaidas around the Sea of Galilee; the other one was designated Bethsaida of Galilee. Bethsaida Julias was named after the daughter of Caesar Julius. Both cities take their names for their principal trade of fishing since Bethsaida means "house of fish."

There is a beach there -- an open area about a mile to the south of the town of Bethsaida -- which was the probable location of this event. It was a secluded area well away from the town itself. There is a hill that gently sloped up away from the sea and in the spring is covered with grass. This spot is called a wilderness spot because it is a significant distance from the city; there is nothing around the area. It is the remoteness of the area that prompted the disciples' early inquiry to send the crowds away so they might make it back to the town for a meal and lodging.

This account of the feeding of the five thousand is the only account (outside of the Passion Week) that all four gospels include in their narrative. John seemed to include this episode not so much because it proves Christ's deity but as a contextual reference point to the sermon he records in the latter part of John 6 -- Jesus' famous "Bread of Life" sermon preached in Capernaum the next day. Jesus knew He must stop this popular uprising to make Him king and giving them the mysteries of the communion supper with no explanation did the trick. The reason Jesus wanted no part of being this group's king was that their motives were impure and it left no room for the crucifixion.

Rest Curtailed
Even though Jesus sought to get away from the crowds, this was not possible for four reasons.

1. The crowds learned of His travel plans

Someone must have overheard one of the discussions between Jesus and the disciples, or one of the disciples must have let slip what they were intending to do.

2. Some saw them leaving

By that time the sail of the boat Jesus and the disciples used would have become familiar to the people. Each boat was different and each sail was distinctive. They could have slipped into the marina area unnoticed; but as soon as that sail was hoisted and moved into the open water, everyone knew who it was. There was only one town in the direction which the boat was pointed, and therefore everyone who was interested would know where He was going -- Bethsaida Julias.

3. Many recognized Him

By this time, Jesus and the disciples were famous in Capernaum and unable to hide their movements. This lack of anonymity seems to have curtailed the ministry of Jesus in the cities. Woe to those who desire to be famous -- it usually becomes a greater yoke than one would like to bear! Anonymity can be a great asset.

Excited about the possibility of spending more time with Jesus, a number of people ran the four to five miles from Capernaum to Bethsaida Julias. This group would have likely been fairly small and physically fit, so it is also likely that there would have been few, if any, who needed healing in this group. It was probably made up of the larger group of the committed disciples, out of which would come "the seventy" later.

The Feeding of the Five Thousand

Imagine the disbelief in the minds of the disciples, possibly even the Lord, when they disembarked in a lonely wilderness spot and found a whole lot of people waiting for them! The vacation was gone. Their rest was over. Think of them in the boat trying to pick a place to berth it. As they aimed for a desolate stretch of beach, a growing band of men began moving swiftly onshore to intercept the boat's harbor. By the time the boat beached and Jesus disembarked, a very large group stretched from this lonely beach south of Bethsaida Julias all the way back to Capernaum. A very great multitude indeed.

It seemed that this group had refused to take the hint that Jesus and the disciples wanted to be alone, but notice Jesus did not revolt in anger for the lack of His private time. Instead He seemed to recognize this as a divine opportunity for ministry. He was overwhelmed with emotion for this diverse group. They moved Him. His compassion was kindled and He could not go away. The truth is that God does not send away the searching heart, even if the search is motivated by the wrong motives.

4. He couldn't ignore their needs

Compassion is a sympathetic consciousness of another's distress together with a desire to alleviate it. Usually compassion is aimed at a particular distress and wells up in the person until there is no option but to help. Jesus saw this multitude streaming towards Him -- four, five, six abreast, stretching for four to five miles. He was struck by the fact that they were leaderless. There was no true religious teacher or governmental leader that was seeking to do God's will at that time. John was the last, and he was just murdered.

Jesus felt deeply the distress of soul that the people could probably not put into words. If you could ask the people about why they were distressed, they might have said a particular illness, lack of money or work, no bread or food for themselves or their family, or the growing Roman oppression. But they probably would not have said, "We are without a leader to guide us into a true relationship with God." Perhaps they had a hint that they needed a leader in their hope for a Messiah, but this would probably not have been the uppermost idea on their mind. But God is constantly in the business of spotting needs in our lives that render us crippled and powerless -- needs we don't even necessarily know we have. These are the needs that must be surfaced and met.

The purpose of the feeding of the five thousand was to highlight the peoples' need for a leader and to make them want Jesus, the Bread of Life. It produced the desired result, however, the problem was that they refused to repent and do what He said. The many problems and blessings that God sends into your life are often designed to raise one's hidden but desperate needs to a level of consciousness. It is God's compassion that moves Him to surface those in your life.

The Multitudes

Jesus took one look at the multitudes and likened them as sheep without a shepherd or leader. Sheep without a shepherd evidence some distinct characteristics as Jesus saw.

1. Sheep with no shepherd constantly wander

These people were wandering from one teacher to the next. Jesus was not the first man to offer Himself as the Jewish Messiah during this period. The book of Acts tells us about one of the false messiahs -- Theudas. The crowds followed each one in hopes that this was the One. Have you been involved in fad teachers and false prophets who spin some radically new version of the Bible or religion? It was no different back then. This tendency to sprint after new religious ideas is devastating to the spiritual life. From Scientology to prosperity doctrines to veiled Hinduism, our generation has this destructive tendency just as the people in the first century did. They were still looking for their true shepherd.

2. Sheep with no shepherd have a herd instinct

Since there was no leader, the whole group moved after itself. These people were following each other. As Jesus saw this group stretched out for miles, surely He must have known that many among this mighty throng were only along because "everybody is doing it." Following the crowd in most things is dangerous but doing so in religion is eternally destructive. The problem with herd movement is that it does not require thinking. It involves no personal decision. If you call yourself a Christian because your parents did or you attend church because your friends do, then this type of unexamined commitment is dangerous. Jesus never let an individual join the group without thinking long and hard about the ramifications of such a decision. Jesus did not want bandwagon followers. Intelligent commitment is the key to a real relationship with God.

3. Sheep with no shepherd have a want of provisions

Sheep by nature do not think ahead and are unable to care for themselves. When they move into a field, they overgraze it and trample their water supply. Likewise this group was just following itself and brought no provisions to sustain its journey. They did not think about the cost such a trip would involve. They just went forward, assuming something would work out in the future and expecting someone to bail them out when they ran into problems from their poor planning.

Thankfully, out of the compassion of Jesus' heart and the power of God, He bailed this impulsive group out of their dilemma. Many today are operating under the same type of impulsive tendencies. They move ahead with little or no thought for the cost or needs of the path they are taking and then expect God to bail them out when they get stuck or get in trouble. Some of the impulsive pathways involve drugs, cigarettes, credit, nutrition, pleasure instead of family, money, sex, etc. The tragedy is that these people demand that God bail them out of the messes they caused by poor planning and yet refuse to submit to His leadership. God is under no obligation to provide goods, services, and healing for the impulsive journey. He may do this on occasion, but we would make a grave mistake to believe that God always will.

Even though Jesus' retreat had been aborted and the rest disrupted, He welcomed those who made the journey to see Him. They streamed toward this wilderness place from many towns and villages, not just Capernaum. The herd instinct had completely taken over.

The large crowd may be attributed to the nearness of the Passover feast. There was free time and the expectation of travel. It's possible that this huge crowd was making their way to Jerusalem for the festival and was free to make this little side trip. This would account for the swelling crowds for many cities.

The Feeding of the Five Thousand

Jesus welcomed the crowd and did two things they expected from Him. He taught them and He healed those who needed healing. The teaching was about the kingdom of God though the particular content of this message is not recorded. The healing was done as necessary as Jesus moved through the groups standing on the grassy knoll. At that point in the ministry the power to heal was such a commonplace occurrence that it received only passing mention in the narrative.

A Hunger Anticipated

The events within this next sequence have been up for discussion for centuries. From the gospel of John it seems best to separate Jesus' interaction with Phillip and Andrew from the later involvement of all the disciples. Without this separation, harmonization becomes increasingly difficult, the text is needlessly twisted, and the insights John shares are lost.

From John 6 we see that Jesus moved up the mountain and took the disciples with Him. As He surveyed the scene He saw a large multitude still streaming in His direction, and He chose to address the food problem. All of the disciples were looking at the crowds wondering what to do about them.

Jesus turned to Phillip and asked Him a question, "Where are we to buy bread that these may eat?" This question was designed to show Jesus' disciples His intention to feed this multitude. The question had no answer except possibly, "Thou knowest, Lord." Some have suggested that Phillip was asked because it is recorded that he was from Bethsaida, but that was Bethsaida of Galilee. It is best to be content that we do not know why the Lord asked Phillip except to stretch his faith. This question is important lest we get the opinion that the only disciples ever addressed directly were Peter, James, and John.

John lets us know that this question was to test Phillip because Jesus already knew what He was going to do. One would think that Phillip and the rest of the disciples would have known that this was the way that Jesus operated after following Him for the better part of two years now. God's tests always come in the form of problems that are too big for us to solve, and this question was too big a problem for Phillip to get his faith around.

Phillip's response was, "Two hundred denarii worth of bread is not sufficient for them." This response is different from the later response of the whole group which was, "Shall we go purchase two hundred denarii of bread?" Phillip puts a monetary amount to the problem -- two hundred denarii. There is always someone in every group who will estimate how much this problem will cost to solve the conventional way. It is conceivable that Jesus knew that Phillip would be the one to ask in order to receive this type of answer.

Two hundred denarii is roughly the equivalent of one year's wages for the workingman. If there are 365 days in a year, and one does not count weekends, holidays, and vacations, then there are about 231 working days in a year. If a denarii is worth about one day's wages, then the amount Phillip suggested equals about what a man could have worked for in one year, rounded off and minus taxes. It seems evident by the way Phillip responded that he did not believe

The Feeding of the Five Thousand

that Judas had that kind of money in the treasury. Jesus' ministry did not run on that type of surplus.

With Phillip's figure and the number of people coming to hear Jesus, his statement that each would only receive a little is very accurate. Solving this problem with a normal monetary solution would result in everyone just having a little. Each person would receive about thirteen percent of a day's wages based upon a crowd of fifteen thousand counting women and children.

Andrew chimed in with knowledge about a lad who wanted to help by donating five loaves and two fish. Andrew seemed to be the most approachable of all the disciples. Of the three times he is mentioned separately in the gospels, he was always bringing someone to Jesus. First, he brought his own brother, Peter; second is this case of bringing this lad to Jesus; and third, he brought the Greeks who wished to see Jesus during Passion Week.

The loaves are barley loaves. This is called "poor man's bread" and was the least edible of all the different types of bread from grain. Barley bread was considered so low that a woman caught in adultery had to bring a barley loaf for a sacrifice. The Pharisees contended that barley bread was not fit for human consumption. It can be hinted that God is not necessarily in the business of tickling our palate but in meeting our needs. The loaves were like pancakes -- round, fairly flat, and small. We are not told this, but I wonder if Jesus made this bread of an exquisite taste as He did the wine when He multiplied it!

The two fish the boy offered were small little fish. They were like the sardines of today. They were pickled to preserve them and were used like a relish to enhance the flavor of the bread. These little fish are the type of meal that Jesus served on the shore after His resurrection when the disciples had decided to go fishing. They had a net full of huge fish, but Jesus had prepared the little fish on the shore surely to harken back to this incident when He proved Himself to be the Bread of Life. He reminded them that they did not need to go back to their old occupations; Jesus would provide.

Andrew's final statement suggested the impossibility of the situation had set in. The money needed to supply this multitude was beyond their reach, and the donations of food amounted to the meager provisions of a little boy and his loaves and fishes.

At this point all the texts suggest that the day was declining. Alfred Edershiem, in his book, *The Life and Times of Jesus the Messiah,* notes that this means it was approaching the end of the first evening. The first evening was from twelve o'clock to three o'clock, and the second evening was from the first star's appearance to the third star's appearance.[2] After the third star, this was considered night. From this description we can conclude that it was about three o'clock.

With Andrew's closing statement and the day declining, there was just enough time for the people to go get food if they were sent away immediately. There might still have been enough time to get the rest and relaxation the disciples needed and consume the five loaves and two fish the boy was willing to leave. This seemed like the ideal solution to the disciples. It solved all the problems. Everyone was happy or so it seemed.

The Feeding of the Five Thousand

An Order Issued

The disciples pressed their case with Jesus: "The place is desolate, and it is already quite late; send them away so that they can go into the surrounding area and get food." The problem with this solution -- which all Twelve seem to have come to agreement on -- is that Jesus was the One who brought up the topic! He wanted to give these people bread. He wanted to provide for this wandering multitude.

Jesus came right back against the disciples' perfect solution: "I don't want the people to go away; I want you to give them something to eat." Jesus issued a series of commands which the disciples seemed perplexed at first to follow.

1. You give them something to eat!

This command was given to put the responsibility for the will of God in this situation clearly upon the disciples. Before Jesus could perform a miracle and strengthen their faith, they must understand that God intended to work through them. They were to be the channel of God's love to this multitude.

The disciples were trying as best they could to follow the Lord's orders, but they were relying upon their own strength and reasoning. They turned Phillip's observation into a formula for carnal faith. Notice they said, "Shall we go and spend two hundred denarii on bread and give them a little something?" Remember that they know there is no money for this type of venture. They were ready to believe Jesus for the wrong thing. They could believe Him for making money, but were unable to believe Him for bread. Imagine if they had gone and executed their plan without checking with Jesus! They would have gone into the local bakery and charged two hundred denarii worth of bread to the ministry. The Lord's ministry would have been in debt, and the people would only have received a small amount of bread. Fortunately they checked with Jesus before they tried to implement their plan for fulfilling the will of God. The method of fulfilling the will of God is as crucial as the accomplishing of it. Christian ministry would do better with more prayer and less barging ahead with what may be the will of God.

2. How much bread do you have? Go look!

This command suggests that the boy who offered his provisions to the work through Andrew was standing a ways off. The disciples must have approached him en masse to examine what he had. Also, they may have checked to see if any other donations had come in. They needed to understand what their resources were.

Jesus wanted all the disciples to have no doubt as to what the starting place was. A miracle is helpful when one understands how impossible it is to start with. Has God put you in a situation where you are becoming aware of how impossible it is to do the will of God with present resources and ability? Rejoice! He probably is getting ready for a miracle.

The disciples returned and reported that the ministry's assets (in terms of food) consisted of five loaves and two little fish. This was not a very big surplus for such a large ministry.

3. Have the multitude recline in groups of fifty

To prepare them, Jesus instructed the disciples to get the crowd to sit down in groups of fifty to one hundred. This process could have been accomplished in only one way. The disciples had to move through the multitude and tell them to sit down on the grass in the groupings. When those in the multitude asked, as surely they did, "Why sit down?" the disciples had no answer for them for they themselves did not have one clue as to what Jesus intended to do.

4. Set these before them!

Before the disciples were given the five loaves and two fish, Jesus lifted His eyes toward heaven and blessed the food that God had provided. This blessing is suggested by Alfred Edershiem, in his book, *The Life and Times of Jesus the Messiah*, as the normal blessing for the evening meal: "Blessed art Thou, Jehovah our God, King of the world, Who causes to come forth bread from the earth."[3] It is possible to believe that Jesus used this common formula, but it is more plausible to believe that He was as spontaneous and innovatively creative in His table thanksgiving as He was in every message He spoke. Also, why would He adopt a formal way of talking to the Father when He was in intimate contact with Him?

The disciples obtained baskets for the distribution process. Most likely these were secured from the crowd as soon as the plan became apparent. These baskets were of the poorest material -- wicker -- but this did not stop Jesus from using them.

Jesus began breaking the bread and handing His provision to the disciples. We are not sure whether it multiplied in the hands of the Savior or in the baskets of the disciples or both. It is not very long until the disciples realized that they had an inexhaustible supply of bread and fish and began handing out as much as anyone wanted. It is evident that the crowd got carried away and took more than they could possibly eat because the disciples gathered up twelve basketfuls of fragments. Imagine the growing confidence of the disciples when they realized that Jesus did not allow them to run out. The truth is that God will not allow us to run out of the things we need in order to do the will of God.

5. Pick up the fragments!

There are three reasons why the Lord would want the disciples to pick up the fragments:

- The Lord was a steward of the resources of the Father. It is not right to waste, abuse, and discard the provisions of God's hand. The wastefulness of the twentieth century church must be called into account. The baskets full of bread could have been distributed to the poor in the next town they were to stop in.

- The Israelites had a penchant for making idols of things connected to miracles. They did it with the bronze serpent of Moses and the ephod of Gideon. Jesus was ensuring that there were not lots of little miracle bread shrines in Palestine. This ridiculous idol worship pulls God's people away from the worship of God in truth. Even today people venerate shrines, splinters of wood, and burial cloths. This reverence is a stumbling block that cripples true reverence for God.

- The disciples had not eaten yet. They had been the servants to the multitudes. These fragments were not crumbs and scraps but uneaten pieces of bread that the eager crowd had taken but unable to consume. This would make a plentiful meal for the disciples on the boat ride back to the other side.

The Feeding of the Five Thousand

Somewhere in the process of picking up the fragments, the truth about what had just taken place leaked out. This led almost immediately to speculation regarding the prophetic identity of Jesus. The crowd was ready to make Him king. After all, anyone who could make bread was worthy to follow. He was the solver of their poverty and work problems. He was the Messiah, their leader.

6. Get into the boat and go to the other side!

This movement to make Jesus king was gaining steam. Jesus had to take care to protect the disciples from the danger that an excitable and massive crowd like this posed. He needed to get them on to the sea where they could not be hassled or harassed.

Having hustled the disciples into the boat, Jesus made His way back through the crowd and departed to a lonely place to pray before the crowd could really get their plans into high gear. Jesus dealt with this notion of making Him king in the sermon the next day -- the Bread of Life sermon.

It had been a day filled with exciting ministry and unexpected events. That evening Jesus needed to retire and He spent considerable time communicating with the Father. It was not until very early the next morning that He walked across the water to get to the other side. If Jesus needed to pray so much, how much more do we need to pray?

Delighting in Jesus

How do we delight in Jesus through the understanding of this episode in the Life and Ministry of Jesus? Jesus does not just teach on the need for faith. He gives exams on faith. He purposely put His disciples in a situation where they would need to trust in Him in a new way. He wanted them to see Him come through. He wanted their faith to grow to handle another challenge. There will be many challenges that come in our lives, and we will be tempted to handle some of them our way leaving everyone broke and exhausted.

Right now Jesus is probably asking you to trust Him for something in your life. It may be about money or about a relationship or about a job. There will be no way to achieve or accomplish the thing that is before you without God stepping in. Trust God and watch your life take a new step forward. If you are going to live on the next plane of spiritual life, you must trust God for something that is beyond you and see Him come through. It is never easy but it is essential. What is God stretching your faith about?

A second way we can delight in Jesus from this passage is to do what Jesus did and get away from the normal soul-sucking routine to rest. On this occasion Jesus and the disciples did not get much rest other than the boat ride, but Jesus initiated the rest period anyway. He didn't just keep plowing forward. He got away with the disciples on a number of occasions far more than I would have thought, given that He knew His ministry was going to only be a few years. Take some time and get away with your family. Rest, change the routine, and enjoy a slower pace.

The Feeding of the Five Thousand

A third lesson that causes us to delight in Jesus is that He was not interested in bandwagon followers. He wanted people to be really committed. Yes, He would heal you. Yes, He would supply bread and meat for you. Yes, He would teach you about God. But He was going to challenge you with some hard sayings. He was going to ask you to trust Him at much deeper levels than the fair-weather followers were comfortable going. Jesus was not trying to get a crowd -- He was trying to get real followers. Sometimes in our Christian walk we come to a place where it is time to move past the shallow faith of the past and push forward to deep commitment. Are you at one of those times? Is God asking you to end a relationship because it is wrong for you and you know it? Is He asking you to get further training for your job or serving Him? Is God asking you to handle your money in a different way than you always have handled it? Is He asking you to grow up in some area of your life where you have consistently acted irresponsibly in the past? Delight in Jesus and go deep with Him.

Chapter 5
Jesus Walks on the Water

Key Verses

Matthew 14:22-33 - *And immediately He made the disciples get into the boat, and go ahead of Him to the other side, while He sent the crowds away. And after He had sent the crowds away, He went up to the mountain by Himself to pray; and when it was evening, He was there alone. But the boat was already a long distance away from the land, battered by the waves; for the wind was contrary. And in the fourth watch of the night He came to them, walking on the sea. And when the disciples saw Him walking on the sea. When the disciples saw Him walking on the sea, they were terrified, and said, "It is a ghost!" And they cried out for fear. But immediately Jesus spoke to them, saying, "Take courage, it is I; do not be afraid." Peter said to Him, "Lord, if it is You, command me to come to You on the water." And He said, "Come!" And Peter got out of the boat, and walked on the water and came toward Jesus. But seeing the wind, he became afraid, and beginning to sink, he cried out, saying, "Lord, save me!" Immediately Jesus stretched out His hand and took hold of Him, and said to Him, "You of little faith, why did you doubt?" And when they got into the boat, the wind stopped. And those who were in the boat worshiped Him, saying, "You are certainly God's Son!"*

Mark 6:45-52 - *And immediately He made His disciples get into the boat and go ahead of Him to the other side to Bethsaida, while He*

Himself was sending the multitude away. And after bidding them farewell, He departed to the mountain to pray. And when it was evening, the boat was in the midst of the sea, and He was alone on the land. And seeing them straining at the oars, for the wind was against them, at about the fourth watch of the night, He came to them, walking on the sea; and He intended to pass by them. But when they saw Him walking on the sea, they supposed that it was a ghost, and cried out; for they all saw Him and were frightened. But immediately He spoke with them and said to them, "Take courage; it is I, do not be afraid. And He got into the boat with them, and the wind stopped; and they were greatly astonished, for they had not gained any insight from the incident of the loaves, but their heart was hardened.

John 6:15-21 - *So Jesus, perceiving that they were intending to come and take Him by force to make Him king, withdrew again to the mountain by Himself alone. Now when evening came, His disciples went down to the sea, and after getting into a boat, they started to cross the sea to Capernaum. It had already become dark, and Jesus had not yet come to them. The sea began to be stirred up because a strong wind was blowing. Then, when they had rowed about three or four miles, they saw Jesus walking on the sea and drawing near to the boat; and they were frightened. But He said to them, "It is I; do not be afraid." So they were willing to receive Him into the boat, and immediately the boat was at the land to which they were going.*

The Story Detailed

Jesus' Intentions
Following the multiplication of the loaves and the fish at

Bethsaida Julias, Jesus was intent on making three things happen. Let's look at each of these to gain a better understanding of what He was trying to accomplish and the significance of this next event.

1. He wanted to get the disciples into the boat and send them to the other side of the Sea of Galilee

Looking at Matthew 14:22-33, there are within this section certain key words that are crucial to investigate in order to get a complete understanding of the text.

Immediately

Jesus put the disciples into the boat *immediately* after they had gathered the baskets of leftover bread and fish. It is suspected that He put them in the boat to protect them from the increasing enthusiasm from the crowd (John 6:14-15). There was no time lost during this process of getting them into the boat and off shore.

Made

The passage says that Jesus *made* the disciples go. This suggests that the disciples did not want to go. They were as excited about the possibility of Jesus as a political king as any in the crowd. Jesus made the disciples get away from this destructive sentiment as quickly as possible. If they were to reduce their faith in Christ to one solely as a political ruler, then they would be unable to cope with their feelings later and His ultimate plan. It is suspected by many commentators that Judas was unable to expand his concept of Jesus beyond a political Messiah and betrayed Jesus when his hopes were crushed.

Jesus' mission was to build a worldwide organization on the strength of these twelve men's commitment to His being God incarnate and the Savior of the world -- the liberator of satanic and fleshly bondage. He could not afford to have them emotionally caught up in the "Jesus-as-King" political party.

Destination

Where did Jesus send the disciples? There are two major theories about their destination. One theory was that they were going to Bethsaida Julias on the eastern side of Galilee near Capernaum, a short distance away from where they were currently. The other theory was Bethsaida, the town south of Capernaum on the west side of the Sea of Galilee.

Some commentators contend that when Jesus told the disciples to head for Bethsaida, he meant Bethsaida Julias. This would have meant that the disciples were to hug the shore and go northwest of where they were. They were to wait for Jesus to finish praying and then meet Him in this nearby city. But the winds were contrary and blew the boat out into the middle of the lake. The disciples struggled for eight to nine hours to try and get to the meeting place but could not. Seeing that they were not going to make the appointment, Jesus needed to go and rescue them and just let the wind blow them to the other side. Those who take this position suggest that it is the best interpretation because:

> 1. If Jesus told them to go across the lake to Bethsaida, then there is no record of their asking Him how He would get there since there was only one boat.

> 2. This would explain why Peter was so bothered by the waves because they would be lashing at him, as the winds would be right in his face.

However, it is far more likely that they went to Bethsaida on the other side. This interpretation suggests that Jesus sent His disciples across the lake to the hometown of Phillip. They started out but were met by a stiff, westerly wind and unable to make any progress toward their goal. After praying, Jesus came to the disciples from the east. When they saw Him, they called out to Him and He rescued them. Then He performed two more miracles: the wind stopped and they immediately reached their destination. The supporting reasons for this interpretation are:

1. There are clearly two Bethsaidas in the gospel narratives: one being designated as Bethsaida of Galilee and the other as Bethsaida Julias or near a wilderness spot.

2. Mark says that the disciples were sent to the other side. Going just a mile up the shore could not be thought of as the other side.

3. John's gospel states that before they had picked up Jesus, the disciples started to head in the direction of Capernaum. This would suggest that they were going to the other side.

4. If the boat were headed west, then the disciples would have been facing east and in the perfect

position to see Jesus approaching from the east. They did in fact spot Jesus a long way from the boat and thought He was a ghost.

5. The topography of the land limits the violent winds to coming from the west. Most often the violent winds come from the west as the desert heat pulls the moist Mediterranean air inland and drops it on the Sea of Galilee some 680 feet below sea level.

The disciples were told to go back in the direction of Capernaum. Jesus did not confide in the disciples how He intended to get back to the town. He could have walked just as the crowds themselves must surely have done. Their final destination ended up being Gennesaret, which is slightly south of their destination. Gennesaret is on the west coast of the Sea of Galilee.

2. He wanted to send the multitudes away

The second intention Jesus had was to send the multitudes away. There are several possible reasons for this:

- *They were a long way from home.* In order to have them make it back to their homes before dark, they had to be sent away during what we would call the early evening. Unless Christ wanted to miraculously provide housing for this mob, He needed to send them away for their own good.

- *They were not eager to leave.* The reality of what had just happened began to dawn upon the multitude, and they did not want to leave. Therefore Jesus had to forcefully dismiss the group.

- *They wanted to make Him king.* This reason is directly stated as a reason for Jesus' withdrawal from the multitudes in John's gospel (6:15). If Jesus did not make the group break up, then the dynamics of a group like that could have combined to make a popular uprising whose goal was to force Jesus to be their leader. This type of mob action is strictly forbidden for the Jew, but it remains a distinct possibility because of the power of the miracle.

- *Jesus wanted to be alone so that He could pray unencumbered to the Father.* It would not have been possible to enjoy uninterrupted peace in prayer with the multitude milling around. He had to send them away. They would surely have followed Him to any remote hideaway if He had failed to make them head in the direction of home.

3. He wanted to get alone and pray

There are some specific things to look at concerning His prayer time with the Father.

Prayer

Jesus' prayer life was constant and focused. He was insistent on getting away and discussing the implications of everything with the Father. There was no hint of His ever taking a "the Father will already know this" attitude or "I don't want to trouble Him with this" or "I am just too tired."

If the pattern of John 17 is any indication, Jesus was probably praying for Himself, the disciples, and the church that was forming. Remember that He as a man was completely dependent upon the direction and power of the Father and the Spirit to live His earthly life. He needed the communication with God the Father and God the Holy Spirit. There is quite a contrastive scene between Jesus praying on the mountain for the disciples to be safe, and the disciples in the boat straining at the oars most likely believing that they would not make it. There can be no greater privilege or security than to have Jesus praying to the Father on your behalf. You are secure whether you feel like you are or not. Jesus has a ministry of shepherding us in prayer in heaven as the book of Hebrews tells us.

Time

Jesus' prayer life was not quick or seldom; it was constant and lengthy. Following the dismissal of the crowds (that may have taken upwards of several hours), Jesus withdrew to pray, putting in a minimum of six hours of engaged prayer time. Jesus' prayers were definitely not rote or a monologue but must have been the most exciting dialogue with His Father in heaven. The range and depth of topics that the Lord covered in that six-hour period must have been fantastic. In our age of speed and shallowness, we tend to draw the line in our relationship with God. We must stop, spend time, go deep, and develop a real relationship. It is unfortunate that most allow the spirit of the day to invade their relationship with the Eternal One.

Mountain

Throughout His ministry Jesus prayed in a variety of different locales and terrain. These varied places point out again the priority that prayer had in the Lord's life. These are a few of the different references to Christ's prayer life -- Mark 1:36, 6:46; Luke 5:15, 16, 9:18, 22:41, 42.

Jesus Walks on the Water

From Jesus' vantage point on the mountain He could look up from prayer and see the disciples quite easily. The moon would have been close to being full since it was near the Passover. The disciples' boat would have most likely been the only boat out on the sea during the storm. The east side of the sea provides numerous peaks from which to view the whole lake. As the wind pushed at Christ's body, He would have known most assuredly that it would push even harder at the disciples' boat.

Alone

Jesus was constantly seen getting away to pray -- even from His disciples. Even though they overheard many of His prayers, they were aware of His need to be away from their ears when He prayed. There can be total honesty when it is just you and God. It is often true that prayer takes on a sanctimonious manner when it takes place in the presence of others. One -- must cultivate a relationship with God alone -- one on one, where no one is trying to be impressed. It is a shame that many have substituted dry, formal prayer or sanctimonious prayer instead of deep honesty with the living God. Honesty is developed alone.

The Disciples' Position on the Sea

There are four observations to make regarding the disciples' position on the sea that are crucial in understanding the miracles that will take place later.

1. The wind

The wind was contrary to the disciples' plans. It was a westerly flow and kept them from making Capernaum or Bethsaida in the normal time. The Sea of Galilee is given to violent storms as its size and depth lends to being whipped up by the waves. Since it is 680 feet below sea level and wedged in between the desert and the sea, violent winds and storms would sweep across it frequently and quickly. With little notice the low pressure in the wilderness would pull the moist air from the Mediterranean Sea with violent force and whip the Sea of Galilee into a cauldron.

2. The method of locomotion

Because of the normal westerly flow across the Sea of Galilee, the disciples would have begun making their way back to Capernaum by tacking back and forth across the lake making progress slowly and deliberately. However, when the violent winds came pouring across the water, the sail would have been no use and potentially dangerous. The oars were the only means of making any headway against the wind and waves. Figuring that there were twelve able-bodied men in the boat, the disciples must have initially thought that the trip across the sea would be routine even with the building wind. But this wind held them in check. They rowed and rowed for many hours and made no headway against it. Their straining at the oars was wearing them out. But the alternative to let the boat be driven and battered by the waves was worse.

3. The fourth watch of the night

The Jews and the Greeks divided the night into three watches of four hours apiece. However, the Romans divided that night into four watches of three hours apiece. It is a picture of the Roman domination that Matthew and Mark designate the time by using the Roman method. The fourth watch was between 3 a.m. and 6 a.m. This means that if the disciples finished cleaning up the fragments of the loaves in the late afternoon and got in the boat about seven o'clock, then they had been in the boat about eight hours having only made about three to four miles of progress. They still had another one to two miles to go which is about four to six more hours at the oars.

4. The condition of the boat

The boat is described as being *battered* by the waves. The word suggests that the wood was stressed and potentially about to break apart which would have thrown its inhabitants into the water. They were really in trouble and had no real way out. Jesus' rescue was a necessary one.

Jesus Walks on the Waves

There are five crucial observations about Jesus' trip across the sea that will further illuminate the passage.

1. The direction from which he came

Jesus was praying on a mountain in the east and the disciples were headed west. While they were rowing, they were in the perfect position to see this form begin moving toward them on the water. It was the fact that they could see Him that frightened them. They actually saw Him walking on the sea! The three-mile walk Jesus took across the lake to where they were would have given them ample time to look, point, discuss, and look again.

2. Jesus' initial intention

According to Mark's account, Jesus intended to walk on by the disciples (Mark 6:48). This distance between Jesus and His disciples allowed them to cry out to Him for help. It seems consistent that Jesus wanted His disciples to seek His help.

If His intention was actually to pass by them, then it could have been that He was going to lead them to shore. This, however, seems unlikely because of what He said to them and its import in the whole context of their lives. It seems best to understand that Jesus would have passed by had they not expressed interest in His helping them. The Lord will often move to deliver or rescue His children but will not do so because they do not really want or ask for His help.

It is a third possibility that Jesus was going to go right on by the boat and go to the other side and then stop the wind, thereby saving the disciples without their direct knowledge. This, however, seems doubtful given the nature of the exchange between the disciples and the Lord. He came so close to them that they exchanged conversation with Him in spite of the noise of the wind and the waves.

Imagine what would have taken place had Jesus not appeared to want to pass by their boat and instead just stalked the boat and climbed in the back with no warning. If He had started to speak without warning, He surely would not have been heard for the disciples would have thrown themselves into the water. Until He reassured them, they were scared to death and wanted to be wherever this "thing" they couldn't identify wasn't.

3. Jesus' appearance to the disciples

The word used to describe Jesus' appearance to the disciples is the word from which we get *phantom*. He appeared to them like a phantom, a ghost, a spirit, or non-corporeal entity. To them it probably seemed that the angel of death was stalking them. As they made their way across the sea and the boat creaked and threatened to break apart, there was a figure slowly following them and coming closer and closer as they strained harder at the oars. It is no wonder that they would be terrified. They probably thought that this could have very well been the end for them.

4. The disciples' reaction

The disciples' reaction involved three things:

- First, they were frightened. This word is *phobao,* or the word for *phobia.* Almost everybody has a phobia about spirits coming after them, and so these men deep in their souls began to believe that their worst phobia (fear) was about to take place. A moon shadow, a spirit, or a ghost was following them.

- The second reaction they had was that they concluded that this thing was a ghost. There must have been a good deal of discussion about what it was as Jesus was walking toward them. They concluded it was a ghost, a phantom. Their mental faculties grabbed a label for this strange phenomenon moving toward them from the stem of the boat.

- Finally, the text tells us that they cried out in fear. This obviously took place when the Lord got closer to them. It is not too difficult to imagine a primordial scream that began building from deep within them and bellowed out as Jesus passed near the boat. Sheer terror and panic seemed to have gripped them. Think of how fast the oars must have been moving at that point!

5. Jesus' words to them

Jesus' words form the most significant part of this whole episode for they seemed to be the key as to why Jesus would put His disciples through this ordeal. He made three statements:

- *"Take courage"* the NASB states, but it is better translated, *"Be comforted"* as it is in the KJV. Jesus, the *paraclete* that He is, had come alongside to help and comfort these stressed victims. One fascinating thing to note is that the stress He came to alleviate had been caused by Him -- at least in their minds. By the time He was by their side, the wind, waves, and boat problems had faded in importance as there was the problem of a ghost alongside their boat. It is a shame that so often Christians mistake God's help as the biggest part of the problem. The Lord is the Master Comforter and knows how to bring comfort and encouragement to His children in the midst of their dilemmas. The Christian has the other Helper, the Holy Spirit, who is with us always.

- *"It is I."* The original Greek translation carries the idea much better and helps explain this whole episode. Jesus replies, *"Ego Eimi,"* which literally means, "I am." Those words, though, were the formula that the Jews in Jesus' day used to designate God. When God gave Moses his name back in Exodus 3:14, it is translated from the Hebrew into the Greek as *ego eimi*. Jesus is claiming, "I am Jehovah, the Eternal One. You can take comfort because of who I am."

The disciples desperately needed to know who Jesus was lest they get caught up in the political movement to make Him king. Jesus was overqualified to be king of a single nation. He is God. They were in danger of limiting the scope and program of God to political power in one small nation. The disciples had to have a lesson they would never forget about who He really is in order to enter into their part of the program and plan of God. They did not catch all of the desire of God here at this juncture, but they did realize that Jesus was no mere political entity, no mere man.

- *"Do not be afraid."* Jesus reassures the disciples that they did not need to be paralyzed by their fear of Him as though He was going to do something to hurt them. It is instructive at this point to note that the fear of the Lord does not involve stark terror or paralyzing fear; it involves reverential awe and trembling at the holiness and majesty of God. We are not to be so afraid of God that we are paralyzed by the very thought of Him. Even though God is an awesome God, we can take Jesus' words at face value -- we do not need to be afraid.

Jesus' words seemed to have had the desired effect as the disciples invited Jesus to get into the boat with them. What a commanding and reassuring voice He must have had to penetrate the terror of their minds and the noise of the storm and to reach in and calm their hearts. His voice still can calm the raging storm in any heart.

Peter's Walk on the Water
The episode with Peter seems to be an interruption to the

main flow of what Jesus had orchestrated and was unnecessary to the point of the story. For that reason John seems to have left it out in possible deference to Peter, his fallen comrade. Peter was dead by the time that John wrote his book. Mark left out the episode most likely because the source of his narrative left it out. (It is commonly assumed that Peter gave Mark the information to write his gospel.) Only Matthew records the highly embarrassing story of Peter's walk on the water and subsequent failure. Matthew was an eyewitness, and we can assume that he was unaffected by any loyalty to Peter and therefore told the tale just as it happened.

There are seven separate occurrences that need to be expanded upon in order to explore the text and the scene more fully.

1. Peter's question to the Lord

Peter understood that this specter was the Lord or at least that it claimed to be the Lord. He forgot himself in relief over the fact that it was not a ghost as they had all thought and sought to join the Lord on the water.

Peter's question can be looked at in two ways. First, it can be viewed as the doubtful but positive faith of an impetuous man. And second, it may be the strong conviction of a man in love with the Lord. These two interpretations hinge on the little word "if" that he uttered, "Lord, if it is you…" Alfred Edersheim, in his book, *The Life and Times of Jesus the Messiah,* suggests that these words denote doubt and some trepidation.[1] William Hendriksen, in his book, *Exposition of the Gospel of Luke,* suggests that it is better to translate "if" as "since."[2] Even though both have validity and probably some measure of truth, it seems best to understand that Peter, for the most part, became convinced that it was the Lord and said, "Since it is you..." This expressed more of a desire to be with the Lord to emulate Him than as a test to prove it was the Lord.

Peter asked Jesus to command Him to come to Him. This meant that Jesus must have been standing on the water some distance from the boat and that Peter's prime motivation was to be with the Lord. If Peter became convinced that Jesus intended to pass by, then he would naturally want to be with the Lord rather than with the disciples no matter what the experience might bring. Peter had this same type of clinginess on the night of the Last Supper when he asked, "Lord, where are you going?" Peter wanted to be with the Lord no matter where. All the disciples demonstrated this quality but none so much as Peter. This single-minded aim to be with the Lord is what proved to be one of his greatest qualities.

2. Jesus' response

Jesus' reply was *"Come,"* one word suggesting that He detected no doubt in Peter at that point. Jesus was always offering open arms to those who would seek to come to Him. "Come to Me, all you who are weary and heavy laden;" "Whosoever will may come." When Jesus calls, we need to come to Him.

3. Peter's action

Peter's action on just one word from the Lord suggested that he was totally convinced it was the Lord. He got out of the boat and began walking toward Jesus. He was not thinking about anything except being with Jesus. Imagine what the disciples must have thought when they saw Peter climb over the side of the boat, stand on the water, let go of the side, and start walking toward the Lord. It is clear that at this time Peter was thinking nothing of it. It is also clear from Jesus' response to Peter's question that Jesus was pleased by this single-minded devotion to Him.

There was no way that Peter could have walked on the water in his own power or that he was aware there was power flowing through him or under him. He was only aware of accomplishing the will of the Lord that had just been revealed to Him. God would supply the necessary elements to make His will complete. Christians need to understand that God will supply all that is necessary to follow Jesus in the service of the will of God.

4. Peter's problem

The reality of what Peter was doing seemed to have set in on him. His focal point was no longer seeking the Lord and doing the revealed will of God; instead he began to focus on the impossibility of the situation. The text says, "seeing the waves and becoming afraid." The waves were most likely hitting him in the lower legs and across his body since Jesus was passing by the boat and the disciples were headed against the wind and the waves. The key idea is that he lost sight of the goal and the power of Christ to accomplish it and began to contemplate the "reality" of the situation.

What is amazing is not that Peter sank but when he began to sink. He was actually walking on water and making headway! In the midst of doing God's revealed will, he ran afoul of fear. Notice that it is fear that killed his faith and therefore the ability to go forward. Peter may have succumbed to fear in doing the will of God, but many never actually attempt the will of God because of fear.

5. Peter's prayer

When he began to sink he cried out, *"Lord, save me!"* At this juncture his fear had completely undermined his determination. He was going nowhere and going down. Prayers that are this direct and to the point are important and get results.

6. Jesus rescued Peter

Jesus immediately reached out His hand to help Peter. This suggests that Peter was not very far from the Lord. We are not told that Jesus carried Peter back to the boat, so he must have walked. We can only assume that he did not take his eyes off the Lord. The touch of the Lord can often reassure those who are sinking beneath the load of their reality.

7. Jesus rebuked Peter

Jesus rebuked Peter for his lack of faith. This may seem harsh, but Peter asked to walk on the water and he was doing what the Lord gave Him permission to do; but he lost faith somewhere in the middle and sunk. Jesus never rebuked His disciples except for lack of faith or lack of belief that God will supply all that is needed to accomplish His will. If we seek permission to do something and He grants us that permission, then He wants us to walk ahead in full faith without doubt or fear of failure. Faith in Christ is always sufficient because Christ is always sufficient. There will always be waves that will threaten to sink us in the midst of the miracle of God's plan, but we must keep our focus on the Lord and let Him take care of the waves.

Final Events

In the concluding sections of the three separate accounts of this miracle, five unique events took place and need further explanation.

1. They took on an additional passenger

Peter's lack of faith made any further thought of walking to the shore impossible, and therefore Jesus got into the boat with them. It is important that we recognize that Jesus does not turn everything into a miracle. This is not a fantasy story where Jesus and Peter float up and fly to the coast with the boat also becoming airborne. Jesus walked on the water, but He also used the normal mode of transportation in the boat after His walk.

2. The wind stopped

Since Jesus was in the boat and the waves were still lashing it, He was no longer unaffected by the wind as He was during His jaunt across the sea. The Scripture says that the wind stopped. In the original text it says that the wind grew weary and ceased. It is important to realize that there was more than one way to overcome the waves and the wind. Jesus, having abandoned the one alternative because of Peter's lack of faith, used another solution -- He just stopped the wind. Jesus has many alternatives at His disposal. He knows all the possibilities of all the possibilities.

3. Inspired commentary

Mark's gospel provides inspired commentary on the astonishment of the disciples. Mark 6:52 states that they had not gained any insight from the loaves and the fish. Jesus could do whatever needed to be done. They were unable to transfer what they knew about the loaves that were sitting at their feet to another impossible situation -- His walking on water. There was a spiritual blindness that lay over even the disciples' eyes as to what was possible through faith in Jesus. They were as yet unable to comprehend what Jesus said would happen.

What seemed to astonish them is not that Jesus walked across the water but that when He said the wind should cease, it did. They were amazed at His power over their natural enemy the wind. Mark's comment suggests that Jesus believed they should have been further along in their belief than they were at this time.

4. The worship of Christ

The final two events of this bizarre night seem to be just as shocking as the rest of that weird morning. After the wind stopped and either before or after they were miraculously transported to the shore (but were still in the boat), the disciples worshipped Christ. It is unheard of for a Jew to worship anyone but the Lord God Jehovah. These men were devout Jews as we can tell by Peter's later refusal to go to the house of Cornelius in Acts 10. The fact that they worshipped Jesus as God meant that they clearly understood whom He had claimed to be with His statement "Ego eimi," and that they became convinced of the truth of that statement by His incredible miracles.

It is significant that Jesus accepted their worship and did not refuse it the way Paul and Barnabas did in Acts or the angel does in Revelation. This story asserts in no uncertain terms that Jesus Christ is the exact representation of the invisible God and is Himself God.

5. An unusual arrival

It is clear from Matthew's gospel that the boat docked along the coast at a place called Gennesaret, which is a little south of where they had set out to end up.

John records the arrival at the shore as another miracle of Christ. As soon as Jesus got into the boat and the wind stopped, the boat was at the land. It is entirely possible that this miracle contributed to the disciples' worship of Christ. John is not given to the use of the word "immediately" as Mark is, so this is not a literary device to move the narrative along but the explanation of an eyewitness. Jesus actually transported the boat and its inhabitants from one to two miles out at sea to the shore in an instant. This follows the mentality of Isaiah 40:31, which says that those who wait on the Lord will mount up with wings like eagles. Patience in the Lord's service is not so much a virtue but an unfair advantage.

Delighting in Jesus

Prayer

Jesus spent considerable time in prayer before He began walking out to the disciples. He was getting instruction about what to do next in this ministry, which was to save the world. It is especially instructive that Jesus, who was God, needed and used prayer more than us mortals. Prayer is essential when it is dialogue. It can be discarded when it is only monologue. For Jesus prayer was clearly dialogue with the Father and the Spirit about everything that was going on in this confining four-dimensional, space-time place called our universe.

Jesus Walks on the Water

Are you asking the Lord Jesus how He wants you to handle tomorrow and then listening for the gentle whispers of His wisdom in Scripture? Are you listening for the Spirit's push back from the plan you just presented? Many times we neglect to pray until after we are in a real difficulty. One of the things that we have been noticing in Jesus' life is that He regularly used the component pieces of the Armor of God spoken of in Ephesians 6:10-18. One of the key ways to build a force field around our life is through dialogue prayer. In this case Jesus made extensive use of the seventh piece of the armor: *prayer*. He needed to get instruction from God the Father and the Spirit in order to proceed with the next part of His ministry. He was to walk by unless they called to Him. We are even in greater need for the wisdom, guidance, power, and grace of God than Jesus, so we must talk with Him.

Too much of our prayer is just one-way conversation with us turning in a requisition list instead of having a dialogue with God about what we should do next. Are you sensitive to the whispers of God in dialogue from His Word? My prayer is that you will get way beyond just asking God for things. You will begin to dialogue with God about your life, your decisions, your relationships, and your problems.

We know that Jesus finished His dialogue with the Father and the Spirit and walked across the sea heading toward Gennesaret. Therefore God the Father and God the Spirit told Jesus to get to the other side of the lake by walking on the water. This was their miracle that He performed in their power. Jesus did not decide to do this. They told Jesus to accomplish getting to the other side this way.

Bring your issues, concerns, and problems to God and then listen to His solultions in His Word. By faith move forward with God's way of living instead of your normal way which doesn't typically work. Welcome the correction and training of God as you move forward with new ways of handling your relationships, your job, your money, your marriage, etc.

Going right on by

Jesus was going to walk right by the disciples who were struggling in the boat. As we see in this episode, God wants you to notice that He is near to you. When Moses was walking in the desert tending sheep, he saw a bush that was burning but was not burned up. The Scriptures say that Moses turned aside to check out this strange phenomenon. Only after he turned aside does it say that God spoke out of the burning bush. In this story Jesus was going to the other side and probably would have walked on by the disciples' boat. He was hoping that they would notice and call out to Him. But if they had not been willing to engage this "ghost" on the water, then they would have not had the faith story we just explored. The lesson for us is when God is near, call out and learn the lesson He wants to teach.

Peter's embarrassment

It is interesting that only Matthew records Peter's failure of faith when he got out of the boat. What are we to make of Peter's passionate inadequate faith? Celebrate it for what it was. He was the only disciple to publicly fail his attempt to walk on water. Peter was the only one of the disciples to actually walk on the water! It is entirely possible that you will fail many times in your attempts to follow Christ in faith. But it is better to attempt to trust God and fail than not to attempt any level of faith at all. Peter is a hero for being so passionate to try to do something that was impossible. When God is pulling at you to go after the impossible, get out of the boat and attempt it.

The loaves at their feet
Jesus rebuked the disciples for their lack of faith. He held them to a high standard of mental understanding. They were sitting in the boat with twelve baskets of miracle bread at their feet, but their faith did not seem to translate from loaves to boat rides. They probably would have done fine if God had been asking them again for the faith to believe that He could multiply fish and loaves. But they had a hard time translating their new found faith in Jesus to multiply loves into making sure that they got to the other side safely. The evidence of God's mercy and grace is all around you. Take notice of them -- especially when God is asking you to strike out in some new direction.

Chapter 6
The Parable of the Sower

Key Verses
Matthew 13:1-23 - *That day Jesus went out of the house, and was sitting by the sea. And great multitudes gathered to Him, so that He got into a boat and sat down, and the whole multitude was standing on the beach. And He spoke many things to them in parables, saying, Behold, the sower went out to sow; and as he sowed, some seeds fell beside the road, and the birds came and ate them up. And others fell upon the rocky places, where they did not have much soil; and immediately they sprang up, because they had no depth of soil. But when the sun had risen, they were scorched; and because they had no root, they withered away. And others fell among the thorns, and the thorns came up and choked them out. And others fell on the good soil, and yielded a crop, some a hundredfold, some sixty, and some thirty. He who has ears let him hear." And the disciples came and said to Him, "Why do You speak to them in parables?" And He answered and said to them, "To you it has been granted to know the mysteries of the kingdom of heaven, but to them it has not been granted. For whoever has, to him shall more be given, and he shall have an abundance; but whoever does not have, even what he has shall be taken away from him. Therefore I speak to them in parables; because while seeing they do not see, and while hearing they do not hear, nor do they understand. And in their case the prophecy of Isaiah is being fulfilled, which says, 'You will keep on hearing, but will not understand; and you will keep on seeing, but will not*

perceive; for the heart of this people has become dull, and with their ears they scarcely hear, and they have closed their eyes lest they should see with their eyes, and hear with their ears, and understand with their heart and return, and I should heal them.' But blessed are your eyes, because they see; and your ears, because they hear. For truly I say to you, that many prophets and righteous men desired to see what you see, and did not see it; and to hear what you hear, and did not hear it. Hear then the parable of the sower. When anyone hears the word of the kingdom, and does not understand it, the evil one comes and snatches away what has been sown in his heart. This is the one on whom seed was sown beside the road. And the one on whom seed was sown on the rocky places, this is the man who hears the word, and immediately receives it with joy; yet he has no firm root in himself, but is only temporary, and when affliction or persecution arises because of the word, immediately he falls away. And the one on whom seed was sown among the thorns, this is the man who hears the word, and the worry of the world, and the deceitfulness of riches choke the word, and it becomes unfruitful. And the one on whom seed was sown on the good soil, this is the man who hears the word and understands it; who indeed bears fruit, and brings forth, some a hundredfold, some sixty, and some thirty."

Mark 4:1-25 - *And He began to teach again by the sea. And such a very great multitude gathered to Him that He got into a boat in the sea and sat down; and the whole multitude was by the sea on the land. And He was teaching them many things in parables, and was saying to them in His teaching, "Listen to this! Behold, the sower went out to sow; and it came about that as he was sowing, some seed fell beside the road, and the birds came and ate it up. "And other seed fell on the rocky ground where it did not have much soil; and immediately it sprang up because it had no depth of soil. "And after the sun had risen, it was scorched; and because it had no root, it withered away. "And other seed fell among the thorns, and the*

The Parable of the Sower

thorns came up and choked it, and it yielded no crop. "And other seeds fell into the good soil and as they grew up and increased, they yielded a crop and produced thirty, sixty, and a hundredfold." And He was saying, "He who has ears to hear, let him hear." And as soon as He was alone, His followers, along with the twelve, began asking Him about the parables. And He was saying to them, "To you has been given the mystery of the kingdom of God; but those who are outside get everything in parables, in order that "While seeing, they may see and not perceive; and while hearing, they may hear and not understand lest they return and be forgiven." And He said to them, "Do you not understand this parable? And how will you understand all the parables? "The sower sows the word. "And these are the ones who are beside the road where the word is sown; and when they hear, immediately Satan comes and takes away the word, which has been sown in them. "And in a similar way these are the ones on whom seed was sown on the rocky places, who, when they hear the word, immediately receive it with joy; and they have no firm root in themselves, but are only temporary; then, when affliction or persecution arises because of the word, immediately they fall away. "And others are the ones on whom seed was sown among the thorns; these are the ones who have heard the word, and the worries of the world, and the deceitfulness of riches, and the desires for other things enter in and choke the word, and it becomes unfruitful. "And those are the ones on whom seed was sown on the good soil; and they hear the word and accept it, and bear fruit, thirty, sixty, and a hundredfold." And He was saying to them, "A lamp is not brought to be put under a peck-measure, is it, or under a bed? Is it not brought to be put on the lampstand? "For nothing is hidden, except to be revealed; nor has anything been secret, but that it should come to light. "If any man has ears to hear, let him hear." And He was saying to them, "Take care what you listen to. By your standard of measure it shall be measured to you; and more shall be given you besides as "For whoever has, to Him shall more be given; and *whoever does not have, even what he has shall be taken away from him."*

Luke 8:4-15 - *And when a great multitude were coming together, and those from the various cities were journeying to Him, He spoke by way of a parable: "The sower went out to sow his seed; and as he sowed, some fell beside the road; and it was trampled under foot, and the birds of the air ate it up. "And other seed fell on rocky soil, and as soon as it grew up, it withered away, because it had no moisture. "And other seed fell among the thorns; and the thorns grew up with it, and choked it out. "And other seed fell into the good soil, and grew up, and produced a crop a hundred times as great." As He said these things, He would call out, "He who has ears to hear let him hear." And His disciples began questioning Him as to what this parable might be. And He said, "To you it has been granted to know the mysteries of the kingdom of God, but to the rest it is in parables, in order that 'seeing they may not see, and hearing they may not understand.' "Now the parable is this: the seed is the word of God. "And those beside the road are those who have heard; then the devil comes and takes away the word from their heart, so that they may not believe and be saved. "And those on the rocky soil are those who, when they hear, receive the word with joy; and these have no firm root; they believe for a while, and in time of temptation fall away. "And the seed which fell among the thorns, these are the ones who have heard, and as they go on their way they are choked with worries and riches and pleasures of this life, and bring no fruit to maturity. "And the seed in the good soil, these are the ones who have heard the word in an honest and good heart, and hold it fast, and bear fruit with perseverance."*

The Story Detailed

The Background

At this point in Jesus' ministry the Pharisees' growing rejection of Him had reached fever pitch. He sought to withdraw from them. However they followed and accused Him of using power from a satanic source to accomplish His work (Matthew 12:14, 24). This accusation was really a rejection by the religious leaders of Jesus as the Messiah, and thus things were different from that point forward.

He had a home in Capernaum that operated as a base camp during His ministry in this region. That day He came out of the house and headed to the Sea of Galilee. When Jesus came out of His house to teach, there would now be a critical change in the direction and preaching of the kingdom. He would no longer be teaching openly without using parables.

Even His mother and brothers were rebuked as to their misunderstanding of His purpose and ministry. He had openly let everyone know that family relations mean nothing in comparison with the bonds that are made with fellow servants of the kingdom of God (Matthew 12:46-50).

Groups of people were streaming toward Him. They came from all different types of cities. Probably most were coming from the cities around the Sea of Galilee but some even as far as Judea. Jesus never ducked any group, and he was about to tell all those there that not all of them were sincere. He had been ministering long enough that the multitude was beginning to splinter into four separate groups -- each group with a separate reaction to His radical message.

Because of the size of the multitude (this was a larger crowd than followed Jesus normally), He got into one of the boats tied up along the beach. He pushed it out to sea and sat down in it.

The crowd remained standing as was customary in that day. They lined up along the whole seashore for quite a distance. Imagine the strength of Christ's voice in order to project to all these people with no amplification system.

Acoustically what Jesus did was very smart in that His voice would bounce off the water much better than had He remained on land. Also this afforded Him the opportunity of facing the whole audience at the same time. It is surmised that in other places the crowds surrounded Him when He spoke.

When Jesus sat down He began to teach them using parables or stories that have a specific meaning. He had never taught exclusively this way before. He had always been straightforward and direct. He explained clearly what He understood the law of the Old Testament to require. He had detailed what He wanted His subjects to do and how to live out the will of God. But very few had really listened. Sure they had been astonished and provoked into deep thought. They had even cheered about how others ought to follow that standard. But very few had really begun to change their lives. Very few had adapted their value system to these incredible positions. So Jesus would not continue to cast His pearls before swine. He told them stories, allegories, and parables which contained the same radical truth; but one must want the truth strong enough to search for the interpretive key. In this way Jesus separated even further those who were only playing at God's will and those who really sought it with all their hearts.

He told them a total of twelve parables that we know of in this first session -- six to the whole multitude and six to the assembled "disciples."

To the crowds by the sea
1. Parable of the Sower
2. Parable of the Seed Growing of Itself
3. Parable of the Tares
4. Parable of the Mustard Seed
5. Parable of the Leaven
6. Many such parables

To the disciples in the house
1. Explanation of the Parable of the Sower
2. Explanation of the Parables of the Tares
3. Parable of the Hidden Treasure
4. Parable of the Pearl of Great Price
5. Parable of the Net
6. Parable of the Householder

Remember, He did not explain anything to them. He just told stories and said, "The kingdom of heaven is like..." and related it to these topics.

The Parable of the Sower
Jesus yelled out, "Listen!" or "Behold!" to signal He was

about to begin the sermon or teaching for the day. This surely gained the peoples' attention and kept them from the idle chatter they engaged in while waiting for Him to start.

He told a story about the sower and his seed. In that day there were two ways to sow seed. The first was by throwing it out by hand and the second by strapping a bag full of seed with numerous holes in the sack to an animal and leading it through the field. It is assumed that the more usual method of throwing the grain out by hand was being referred to in this instance.

Jesus' opening statement would have immediately created a picture in the minds of the audience -- a rich and fertile field with a road passing by on one side, a hedge fence on the other, and a portion of the field on top of a rocky knoll. This was a common picture to the people standing on the seashore that day.

Jesus' point was to highlight the type of soil or ground that the seed would find when it left the sower's hand, so He ignores all the other parts about the scenery and topography. We are not told about water, shade, wind, climate, or the landowners. The soil was the point and He zeroed in on that alone.

Jesus first mentioned that some of the seed would fall on the side of the road or right next to it, where the plow had not reached. It would have been trampled hard by occasional traffic. It was not the road He was talking about but the *side* of the road. Jesus very rarely declares that a person is unredeemable; He usually suggests that a person is very close to being in a condition where there is no recovery. The roads

The Parable of the Sower

in that day (other than the Roman highways) would have been well-worn dirt strips packed hard by the constant traffic. When a wagon or herd of sheep passed along it there was never any guarantee that they would stay right in the road, but they might step on and harden the sides also.

Next Jesus talked about the seed among rocky soil. This does not mean that the soil had rocks mixed all through it, but that it was soil over the top of rock. The land of Palestine is dotted with rocks and much of the fertile soil is laid over the tops of these rocks. There is not much soil over the rock, and the roots of any plant cannot dig deep for water. There is only one way to go for seed planted in this type of soil -- up.

The lack of a deep root system in this type of soil made those crops extremely susceptible to burning. The sun would literally cook these plants because they had only the water that the exposed portion could hold. This type of soil was only good for planting during part of the year. If the crops weren't harvested before the heat of the summer, then they would be gone.

The third type of soil over which the sower spreads his seed is thorny soil. This is not soil with thorns already in it. It would be ridiculous for the sower to throw good seed into a thorn patch. But this is soil that looks like good soil. It is plowed and cultivated. It looks clean and ready to receive the new seed, but underground the soil is infested with the roots and seeds of thorns and briars. The roots and seeds of these weeds are undetected until the farmer begins to apply the water to irrigate the seed he has planted in the field. The water activates the briar seeds and thorn roots. Since weeds always seem to multiply faster than that which is beneficial, the thorns weave a dense net of roots around the seed below the ground that rob the good seed of the needed nutrients, effectively choking it out.

Above ground the process is similar only slower, and has less to do with the final outcome. It is only after the field is growing that the farmer can tell what the thorns have done, and by then it is too late. The thorns have destroyed the fertility of the good seed. The seed tries to send its new life heavenward, but it never gets all it needs and is left weak and neglected before an ever-growing menace.

Jesus' last soil type is good soil. There were various types of good soil, but Jesus here described it as soil that produces at least a thirty-fold increase. This means that the amount of seed that is sown in it is returned and thirty times more. This is the bare minimum that Jesus called good soil. There were some good soils where the nutrients were plentiful and the yield was sixty times the amount of seed put into it. And then there was the type of soil where the climatic conditions, the nutrients, the water, and other factors were just right to produce a bumper crop of one hundred times the amount of seed put into that field. Every farmer desired to have that type of field.

All these types of soil were known to this largely agrarian society. Even the fisherman would know of these different types of soil for they would have grown up around the farmers inhabiting the low-lying countryside, and they would have done business with farmers who were owners of all different types of soil.

The Parable of the Sower

Jesus finished this first parable with the statement, "He who has an ear to hear, let him hear." This seemed to be one of Jesus' favorite sayings, goading His listeners to seek out the message behind the story. He was also saying that some of those listening did not have ears to hear. They had stopped listening. He repeated this instruction here in Mark 4:23, 8:18; and Revelation 2:7, 11, 17, 29, 3:6, 13, 22.

What did Jesus really want these people to hear in this parable? They were in charge of the condition of their soil (soul). He was telling them that some of them were hard, some were shallow, and some were too consumed with the world; but a few were ready for God's work in their hearts. Remember that Jesus had just finished delineating the unpardonable sin and the blasphemy of not allowing the Holy Spirit any room in their life to witness to the truth of the person of Christ. What He is really saying is that we are in charge of our level of receptivity to God. Some of us have not tended our souls, and it is leading towards the unpardonable sin -- not responding to the whispers of the Spirit of God.

The Disciples Questioned His Method

Jesus dismissed the crowds and moved back to His rented quarters. Maybe He just got up and rowed the boat ashore and walked through the crowd to His house -- this being the signal that He was done speaking publicly even though He had only told a few stories.

Once He was alone, the disciples (which included the Twelve and a good number more) began peppering Him with questions. We know that they asked at least two:

- Why do you speak to them in parables?
- What does this parable (referring to the sower) mean?

They most likely asked more questions but we have no record of them. The inference is that they asked Jesus about the meaning of all the parables that He had told to the crowd. Jesus replied to their first question and it is recorded in Matthew. It is important to realize that God inspired Matthew to record the crucial answer to the first question and the meaning of the parable of the sower. While Jesus most likely had a much more wide-ranging discussion with the disciples, the answers that we desperately needed to know are recorded in the Scripture.

The Reasons for Parables

Jesus told them that they had been privileged to know the mysteries of the kingdom and that knowledge had not been granted to the crowds. Before we become upset by Jesus' exclusion, we must understand that one could become a disciple of Jesus by his or her own choice. It was their willingness or lack of it that determined whether they would hear the greatest teacher of all time delineate the mysteries of the kingdom.

The word *mystery* means a person or a truth that would have remained unknown had God not revealed it. There are many mysteries of God's plan that were hinted at before but are now brought out into the light in the New Covenant. Some of these are:

- The Jewish nation as a whole was being hardened, with only a remnant remaining true to God, while the Gentiles were to be saved. (Romans 9-11)

- Some who believe in Christ will not all die. Those fortunate few who are alive when Christ returns will be caught up into the clouds to meet the Lord without dying.

- Christ Himself would actually dwell in the hearts of those who were believers in Him -- both Jews and Gentiles.

- Certain details about the man of lawlessness -- the Antichrist.

Also, Jesus was going to tell His disciples things about the kingdom of God that had never been revealed before. They had the privilege of hearing details about the kingdom not even considered before.

The passages directly record Jesus' amazing statement in explaining why He spoke to the multitudes in parables. *And He was saying to them, "To you has been given the mystery of the kingdom of God; but those who are outside get everything in parables, in order that 'While seeing, they may see and not perceive; and while hearing, they may hear and not understand lest they return and be forgiven.'"* Jesus said that certain people had proven to be more receptive to spiritual things, and they were given more understanding. The truth revealed in the Parable of the Sower is the reason why Jesus spoke to the people in parables. The stories weeded out those who really wanted to know from those who just wanted to be entertained, fed, or healed. Those who responded to the whispers of God's Spirit received more information and more insight into the things of God.

Jesus made the further statement that He spoke in parables because "seeing they do not see, and hearing they do not hear." What he meant is that when He gave them the straight stuff, they did not use it or understand it. When He told them how to straighten out their messy lives, they did not act upon it. They didn't want to change or they would not have treated these precious truths with such contempt. So they did not deserve to know the further truths about the details and nature of the kingdom. Their lack of moral virtue and diligence rendered them useless, and who knows what they would have done with the truths of the kingdom if they were to hear them. Potentially they would have twisted them into some perverted shadow of their reality.

Jesus quoted a prophecy of Isaiah and let the disciples know that these people who refused to really listen to what He said were fulfilling the words spoken by the prophet some eight hundred years before. Their hard hearts and dull hearing had rendered God no choice but to judge them unworthy of hearing the reality of the message of redemption and release.

Jesus took the time to answer their first question to let them know He considered them blessed because they had appropriated the truth by changing their lives accordingly. They really heard the message and acted. They had made themselves good soil.

The really strange thing about this private meeting and explanation with the disciples is that there were all kinds of disciples present. Surely there were no "beside-the-road" type of believers, but there were most assuredly the other three groups represented among the people He was with. Only one of the three groups would have the seed that became truly profitable so that they would gain the maximum benefit from it. Only one group of the three that made up the multitude of disciples would inherit eternal life. As it says in John 6, many of His disciples no longer walked with Him because they found His sayings too difficult (6:60-66). Jesus had at that point weeded out the really hardhearted of the multitude and there were other "weedings" to come.

He let those gathered in the house know that they really stood in the place of privilege. Any number of prophets would have given anything to stand where they were standing -- in the private conversation of the Messiah. Think of Abraham, Moses, Isaiah, Jeremiah, Amos, Habakkuk, and even John the Baptist of that day. The disciples stood at the head of a privileged group. Don't blow your chance!

The First Parable Explained
The second question the disciples asked was answered in the lengthy explanation of the first parable. Jesus did not explain all the parables He told, but He did get the ball rolling with a lengthy discourse on this first parable. He gave them the interpretive keys so they could completely grasp its meaning. Remember that understanding is not the end of the reason for this parable. Action is Jesus' ultimate goal. If they truly understood it and grasped its significance, then they would

strive to make themselves good soil -- *people in which the Word can make the most progress.*

Even though Jesus' point was to spur the disciples to action, He did not explain how to take the action. He did not give them specific instruction on what they should do to make sure they avoided the problems He discussed.

Jesus shared the key interpretive explanation when He said, "The seed is the Word of God." It is crucial to understand what the seed is. Only when we fully understand what the seed is will we be able to let it have its perfect way in us. Many have suggested that the seed is completely encompassed in the forgiveness of sins through Jesus Christ's death on the cross. This would make the multiplication process simply sharing with others the forgiveness of sins. Fruit is then reduced to converts. But Jesus says the seed is the Word of God, the whole complete teaching about the will of God that He was explaining to His disciples. The seed implanted in people is so much more than the truth of forgiveness of sins, although that is a place to start. It is all the things Jesus taught. He says this in Matthew 28:18-20, *"...teaching them to observe all that I have commanded you..."* Multiplying the seed which Jesus sows means letting His teaching take hold of every part of your life and reflecting the image of Christ.

The disciples never saw the Christian message as one of simple belief but as complete commitment to a lifestyle. It begins in belief, but it transforms the life or else it is bogus belief. We must return again to sowing the full seed lest we continue with this incredibly weak strain of wheat; so weak in fact, that it seems doubtful that our Lord would recognize it as a field of wheat at all.

The First Soil

The first soil is explained as those who hear the words of the kingdom but it makes no penetration into their lives. Jesus said they do not understand it. By that He meant that they failed to even consider the changes necessary to live this type of lifestyle.

As a judicial punishment for their hardheartedness, the Evil One comes and snatches away the Word. These are people who don't even have to work at thinking of something to replace the thoughts of devotion to God they may have just heard -- the Devil does it for them. The Devil dispatches an emissary to make sure the unbeliever stays blind (2 Corinthians 4:4).

There is no condemnation to the permanence of this position. It is possible that they could be made into good soil, but the chances are very remote. They are the furthest from real receptivity to the message of Christ.

The Second Soil

The second type of soil is identified as thin topsoil over rock. This type of soil represents people who are temporary believers. They do not prepare enough of their lives for the receptivity of the gospel. They seem to make the most progress or give the most outward evidence of change early on, but the penetration of the gospel is superficial. The slightest affliction or persecution leaves them abandoning ship. These people look religious but they are oak veneer over pressboard, chrome over pot metal -- all show and no go.

What is interesting is that Jesus condemned this group even though they gave lots of early evidence of a changed life. His evaluation is based upon the depth of their commitment to Christ and the amount of fruit they produce. In making Christians (disciples), as well as growing crops, one is not looking for vegetation but production. A cornfield can be condemned no matter how high the stalks are if all the ears have no corn. Many need to examine their lives to see if they are full of religiosity but exhibit no real change. Are they full of bumper stickers, necklaces, literature, and music but have no love, humility, submission, peace, and forgiveness? Jesus is after yield.

Affliction means to suffer persistent pain or distress. Persecution means to harass in a manner designed to injure, grieve, or afflict. These people are wilted by the fact that they are becoming different and others are noticing it and pointing it out. These folks want no pain in their lives. They are the electricity of religion bowing in whatever path is that of least resistance. Heat from the sun wears on any crop but on this group it destroys it. Perseverance through thick and thin is the mark of the Christian.

In an agrarian society hot summer sun is the bane of a good year just as too much rain is the bane of a leisure-oriented society. "Into every life a little rain must fall" is how we would say it. Jesus says it, "Into every life a little sun will shine." The question is the same -- have you gone deep enough to handle it?

Marriages are predicated upon commitment through thick and thin, and God demands this same type of commitment when it comes to following Him. Why would He allow less commitment than we would give to another human? The answer is He doesn't.

The Third Soil
The third type of soil is thorny soil—soil that looks good but is infested with the seeds of its own destruction. There are people, Jesus says, who look like they are committed and yet will be driven out (or choked out) of their love for Christ by the worries and cares of the world.

To be choked out is to die in stages, incrementally losing one's ability to sustain life. It is different from doing immediate irreparable damage to a life. At any stage in the choking process the person can rationalize that it can be turned around and nutrients given to the starving relationship. What is usually accomplished is that one does not seek to reverse the damage until the relationship is dead. It is at this point that the reversal process in which so much hope was placed is useless. The life is dead. Many starve their relationships with God for years telling themselves that they will get back to church and the Bible in a little while. They just have to concentrate on whatever commitment occupies them at the present. Then when their relationship with God is really dead, they venture back to church or prayer or the Bible but fail to sense the life they thought was there before. Then it is concluded that there is no reality to this religion stuff or that they have outgrown their need for God.

This is a disciple who has a divided heart. He has a love for Christ and a receptivity to change that Christ naturally brings, but he also has three very virulent enemies at work within him—*worry, riches, and desire for material possession.*

- Worry assumes responsibilities God never intended you to have. It is mental distress or agitation resulting from concern, usually for something impending or anticipated. These people run afoul of the number of potential disasters to the things in their lives: car accidents, kidnapping, thefts, fires, accidents, lawsuits, etc. -- all the potential things which could happen and cause them to lose prestige, possessions, or power. All the mental power that is diverted to these thoughts is robbing God from His use of their mind and spirit.

- Riches are said to be deceivers. They promise what they cannot deliver. We can quickly be consumed with pursuing them in order to have what they promise; and they take away our time, energy, and focus from God. Many who are caught up in this game cannot even tell you why they want more except that everybody does, or they cannot tell you when they will have enough. Checking the stock sheet or investment portfolio more than God's glint of approval will eventually result in the will of God becoming a distant memory. Jesus says that you can't serve both money and Go. You are going to have to choose.

- Possessions come with the responsibility to maintain them. It is this growing list of duties that Jesus says eats away at the commitment one makes to Christ and renders it weak and sickly. If the number of things is not minimized, then one's commitment to Christ will die. One often sees the person who gives his life to Christ and then begins to reap the benefits of time spent near God. These benefits become the focus for the person instead of the God who gave them. Now notice it is not just the possessions that Jesus says will rob you of the multiplying effect of the Word of God but the desire for more possessions will as well. It is the carrot ever in front of you that keeps you from looking at where you are. In a day of advertising, one must be careful not to follow the lure of products into a cul-de-sac of dead relationships -- especially regarding our relationship with God.

Unfortunately Jesus lets us know that these three maladies will destroy the fledgling commitments of some who have begun their journey to the celestial city.

The Fourth Soil

The fourth type of soil is the type that Jesus is after. It is good soil, ready for maximum output and production. The Word of God falls into these people's lives and does not lie dormant or die from other suitors for nutrients. Instead it flourishes and multiplies. These people change and it is obvious.

It is crucial to notice that it is only this last type of soil that really understands the ramifications of the gospel message. It is not something to be isolated into some little religious compartment, but it is to transform the whole life. Jesus Christ comes into the life as Lord and Savior. Just as a field matures over time and in different sections at different rates, so does the Christian's permeation with Christ's Lordship. But there is willingness and most often evidence of His work.

Each person will produce a different amount of the qualities and character of the kingdom, but Jesus commends all who multiply the fruit of the kingdom.

It is unclear as to whether Jesus was suggesting that of the three different types of good soil, it is possible for everyone to become like the one hundred-fold soil. It is best to fall back upon Jesus' clearer statements when in doubt like this. He stated unequivocally in the parable of the talents that any person who produces with the talents given Him receives a "well done." Therefore, it is not wise to suggest that there are progressive amounts of harvest in the growing Christian.

Delighting in Jesus

Sensitize your soul to be more receptive to God's Word. Examine what type of soil you are. Are you receptive to the things of God, allowing the Word of God to go deep? You can become that way! Make the necessary choices to embrace Jesus and His Word and your soil will change from hard, shallow, and thorny to deep, rich, and spiritual. You can have a different life by inviting the Living Word of God into your life in a deeper way. Are their areas of your life where Jesus is not really welcome? Invite Him into those areas.

Chapter 7
The Problem of Tragedy

Key Verses

Luke 13:1-9 - *Now on the same occasion there were some present who reported to Him about the Galileans, whose blood Pilate had mingled with their sacrifices. And He answered and said to them, "Do you suppose that these Galileans were greater sinners than all other Galileans, because they suffered this fate? "I tell you, no, but unless you repent, you will all likewise perish. "Or do you suppose that those eighteen on whom the tower in Siloam fell and killed them, were worse culprits than all the men who live in Jerusalem? "I tell you, no, but unless you repent, you will all likewise perish." And He began telling this parable: "A certain man had a fig tree which had been planted in his vineyard; and he came looking for fruit on it, and did not find any. "And he said to the vineyard-keeper, 'Behold, for three years I have come looking for fruit on this fig tree without finding any. Cut it down! Why does it even use up the ground?' "And he answered and said to him, 'Let it alone, sir, for this year too, until I dig around it and put in fertilizer; and if it bears fruit next year, fine; but if not, cut it down.'"*

The Story Detailed

In the center section of Luke, Jesus deals with a number of interesting and thorny issues. These include the Good Samaritan, the Prodigal Son, the problem of tragedies, and the inevitability of stumbling blocks. Let's look closely at Luke 13:1-9 to see Jesus' perspective.

"Now on the same occasion..."
Jesus' discussion regarding the problem of tragedy occurred at the same time He was discussing the signs of the times with the multitudes which was different from that in Matthew 16:1-4. This discussion hinges not on the inability of the Pharisees and Sadducees to discern the presence of their Messiah but on the multitude's inability to understand and carry out basic righteousness. Jesus states in Luke 12:57, *"And why do you not even on your own initiative judge what is right?"* In other words, you are so good at deciphering the weather, but you are totally ignorant in terms of basic righteous behavior. Jesus utterly condemns the people for sinfulness.

It is Jesus' implied condemnation of their sinfulness that provides the backdrop for His discussion involving the problem of accidents and tragedies. This, then, forms the context around how Jesus deals with the report of the Galileans killed by Pilate.

"...there were some present who reported to Him..."

The key word in this phrase is *reported*. It suggests that the people who came and relayed this information to Jesus did not do it in a hostile or questioning tone. They were merely detailing the current events. They may have been seeking a reaction or commentary from Jesus, but there is no hint in this word that the question was designed to challenge or trip Him up. Jesus' reply suggests that He took their report and their desire for inspired commentary and put a new spin on their normal mental processes. Jesus followed up His discussion of their utter sinfulness (in the signs-of-the-times talk) with a heavenly perspective about two recent tragedies.

"...about the Galileans..."

The Scripture clearly declares that the men involved in this incident were Galileans. We are not told what sin they committed or in what way they outraged Pilate. Calvin insists on calling these men Samaritans to explain the Jews' superior opinion. Alfred Edershiem, in his book, *The Life and Times of Jesus the Messiah,* states that these men were no doubt zealots whose open political aspirations for the nation of Israel put them in rebellion with Rome.[1] Some have suggested that they are specifically referred to as Galileans to elicit a hometown sentiment in Jesus and produce a denouncement of Pilate and Rome in this way. The problem with all these interesting theories is that they have not an ounce of Scriptural evidence. Remember that the incident was simply reported, not used as a question. It is also important to note that even if the report were trying to be used as a sentimental provoker, Jesus slid by the issue and mentioned the accident that occurred to Jews living in Jerusalem.

It is best to regard this as a news items Jesus learned of that day which He chose to use to make His point about the utter sinfulness of people and the absolute need for repentance.

"...whose blood Pilate had mingled with their sacrifices."
William Hendriksen, in his book, *Exposition of the Gospel of Luke,* reports "Pontius Pilate was the fifth procurator of Samaria and Judea. He was under the authority of Syria's legate."[2] Many reports have come down to us about him. Estimates of his character range all the way from that of Philo, who, quoting a letter from Agrippa I to Caligula, calls Him 'inflexible, merciless, and obstinate,' a man who repeatedly inflicted punishment without previous trial and committed ever so many acts of cruelty; to that of the Cops and Abyssinians who rank him among the saints! One thing is certain: he exercised little common sense in handling the delicate problem of the strained relations between the Jews and their Roman conquerors. In fact, it would almost seem as if he enjoyed denouncing the Jews: using the temple treasury to pay for an aqueduct, bringing Roman standards into Jerusalem, and even defiling the temple with golden shields inscribed with the images and names of Roman deities.

The occasion that later led to Pilate's removal from office was his interference with a mob of fanatics who, under the leadership of a false prophet, were at the point of ascending Mt. Gerizim in order to find the sacred vessels which (as they thought) Moses had hidden there. Pilate's cavalry attacked them, killing many of them. Upon complaint by the Samaritans, Pilate was then removed from office. He started out for Rome in order to answer charges that had been leveled against him. Before he reached Rome, the emperor

(Tiberius) had died. An unconfirmed story, related by Eusebius, states that Pilate 'was forced to become his own slayer.'"

What obviously took place in the account before us in Scripture was that certain Galilean Jews came to offer sacrifices either for sin or for a feast. In the midst of their sacrificial offering, the Roman army stormed through the Court of the Gentiles and cascaded across the court of the women into the temple square, where only Jewish men were allowed. Once in the temple square, they saw the fugitives (who may have assumed they were safe in the temple area) offering sacrifices. In the midst of making their sacrifices these men were grabbed, held, and slain -- the twelve-inch blades of the Roman soldiers ripping huge holes in the writhing torsos of the men. The insides of these men would have spilled out on to the ground, mixing their own blood with the blood of the slain sacrifices they had brought. Their blood had literally been mixed with the blood of their sacrifices.

This violently horrific scene was reported to Jesus and formed the backdrop for His urgent plea that everyone should repent. It is amazing that the cruel, violent massacre of fellow Galileans would elicit from Jesus the cry for repentance. However, that is only because we do not understand Jesus' thoughts about the holiness of God's character and divine justice.

Sacrifices
It has been suggested that Galileans would have been in Jerusalem and in the temple area for two reasons only: First,

to celebrate some feast for Galileans did not make the long trek to Jerusalem except on one of the three major feast days; and second, to offer sacrifices for their sins.

If both of these ideas are combined with Jesus' remarks about the men's sinfulness (and the lack of rancor regarding Pilate in the report suggests that they should be) then only one particular feast could satisfy both elements of this story. The only feast in which the major emphasis is upon sacrifice for sin is Yom Kippur and the Feast of the Tabernacles. It is possible that these Jews made the trek to Jerusalem in late September or early October to be cleansed from their sins and were killed during this time. This particular chronology fits the center section of Luke that would have Jesus heading toward Jerusalem during the last six to nine months of His ministry, staying often near Jerusalem in the Perean wilderness.

"And He answered and said to them…"
Jesus took advantage of this particular report to pick up where he left off on the topic of righteousness and their inability to recognize it. Jesus is the One who initiated the volatile nature of this conversation. He gave an answer when there was no real question. The Lord often initiates controversy when there was none intended in order to drive a particular point home.

"…Do you suppose…"
Jesus knew the mental reasoning the Jews were going through to explain away the problem of a tragedy like this one. Jesus suggested that their way of thinking about the

problem was completely wrong. They were unable to apply this tragedy to their lives correctly because they thought about tragedy incorrectly. We, too, shield ourselves from God's thoughts and applications by incorrect mental ruminations. We do not begin in our thinking about tragedy realizing that we are sinful creatures, constantly rebelling from God's way of living. Every minute of our life is a gift from God.

"...that these Galileans were greater sinners than all other Galileans because they suffered this fate?"

The common Jewish perspective on this particular tragedy seemed to be that these men's sins were so great that while they were offering sacrifices God saw to it that Pilate came and executed the divine sentence upon them. It was the Jews' reasoning which led to Jesus' reply: God's reason for allowing them to be destroyed in this manner was not that they were more heinous than all other Galileans, but rather that being sinners like all other Galileans God chose to exact the death penalty at that point in time.

The Jews accurately discerned that God operated on the basis of cause and effect. However, they failed to see the real cause of fatal tragedy—man's sin. In order to account for episodes like this one where people were slaughtered heinously, the Jews came to believe that it could only mean that God had detected some hidden sin that required He take their lives. They failed to understand two ideas that Jesus pointed out.

1. *All men are sinners.* Jesus pointed out that all men are sinners and that there is no such thing as innocent people. All men are born with a sin nature in rebellion to God. All men sin and prove their rebellion with

outward acts of defiance. Although there are different types of sins, sin is still full rebellion against God's standard.

2. *All sins carry the penalty of death.* Most people look at the Old Testament as more harsh than the New Testament in terms of the death penalty for the death penalty is listed for numerous crimes in the Old Testament while there is no such list in the New Testament. What often escapes the notice of the Old Testament student is that these laws were a gracious extension from God's original law which was this: *the soul that sins, it shall die.* All sin in Genesis 3 carried with it the death penalty. It was only God's grace extended to Adam and Eve's lives that allowed them time to repent.

When God originally put the universe together, He created man to live in harmony with Himself, a Holy God. There could be no aberrations from His holy standard. He let Adam and Eve know that the day they ate from the Tree of the Knowledge of Good and Evil, they would die. There was no promise of gracious delay in the sentence, only sure execution. It was because of God's mercy and grace that He did not immediately execute Adam and Eve but allowed them time to repent and continue existing.

God instituted the principles and laws for man to use to construct a society where mankind shall govern themselves and live in harmony as a society. In His sovereignty He stated that a number of sins should carry the death penalty. It is important to note that these were not laws designed to allow man to live in harmony with a Holy God, but instead were designed to allow man to live in harmony with each other within a society. The following is a list of the Old Testament's laws that required the death penalty:

- Striking or cursing parents
- Desecrating sacrificial offerings
- Murder
- Kidnapping
- Idolatry
- Child sacrifice
- Blasphemy
- Sabbath violations
- The practice of magic
- Consulting mediums and wizards
- Unlawful divorce
- Homosexual practices
- Incest
- Bestiality
- Prostitution of virgins
- Rape
- Practicing false prophecy
- Refusing to obey the verdict of a priest-judge
- Bearing false witness in a capital case
- Stealing for slavery

When God sought to outline the principles and laws that would need to be in place for an individual to live in harmony with another individual, the death penalty is rarely mentioned. This is the thrust of the New Testament's ethical teaching—individuals living in harmony with other individuals. In fact, forgiveness is the consistent thrust in the gospels and the epistles. It is clear from certain passages in the New Testament (Romans 13, 1 Corinthians 6) that the methodology of forgiveness will not work on a governmental or society-wide basis.

It seems clear from Jesus' question that the Jews believed two concepts that do not stand up under the scrutiny of Scripture and were therefore erroneous:

1. *All men are entitled to a certain number of years of life.* The usual life span was three score and ten as stated by Moses. The fact that this was the typical amount of time one spent upon the earth gave rise to the belief that one was owed this amount of time. It is assumed then that one must have done something very sinful to be robbed of this expected life span. Modern day critics would add that God must be a terrible or evil God to rob the innocent of one's expected lifespan.

2. *God views sin just as man does.* Every man labors under the sentence of death for his sin. Each sin he commits adds another degree of death -- a forfeiture of life. More importantly, it renders him incapable of dwelling with a Holy God. The Jew came to feel that the laws God gave to the Israelites to govern their relationships with each other and with Him as their God was how He reacted to sin. They came to

identify certain sins as capital offenses in God's eyes and others as only minor offenses. What is clear is that sin in any form -- down to the smallest aberration from the norm of God -- immediately merits His wrath and demands His justice—forfeiture of life. Sin in any form is a capital offense to God.

"I tell you, no, but, unless you repent, you will all likewise perish."
Jesus seeks to drag our thinking back to reality by showing us that we are all under a death sentence. God is going to execute all of us. No one escapes the sentence of death, so what does it matter if the only variable is a few years difference in the date? Jesus would have us remember that the ultimate absurdity is death. We all have the immortal within us. It is this immortality that we are effacing when we suggest that death at seventy or eighty is more normal than death at twenty or fifteen. Death at any age is a violation of who we were made to be.

It would be ridiculous for two death row inmates to conclude that they were better or more acceptable than two other inmates who had been executed the day before simply because their date of execution had not yet been set. Yet this is the type of sloppy thinking that the Jews were engaged in. Jesus let them know that they would all perish and the only hope was repentance, throwing themselves on the mercy of the court and changing their minds and behavior in regard to their rebellion.

The Jews had rebelled against God's laws in numerous ways even while they proclaimed loudly that they were the keepers of the Law. They found every little rationalization to go around the law of God to work their selfish ways. Even greater was this group's sin in refusing to accept Jesus as the Messiah and the Son of God. These people were sinners but were also rejecting the only Advocate and Sin-bearer that the Sovereign Judge was providing.

"...unless you repent..."

The word *repent* means "to change one's mind." It comes from two Greek words *meta,* which means "after," and *noied,* which means "to think." Therefore, it carries the idea of "to think after" or "to change one's mind." Repentance must result in a corresponding change in behavior, or the mind has not truly changed. This group must repent in at least three areas:

1. They must repent or change their minds and behavior in regard to God's laws. No longer can they go on deluding themselves with half-hearted obedience and insincere devotion.

2. They must repent or change their minds from the arrogant way it works. They used their minds to reason why they were superior to others instead of realizing that, except for the grace of God, there go I.

3. They must repent or change their minds from the way they perceive Jesus. They must wholeheartedly follow Him and quit this cautious and doubtful questioning of His person and work.

Jesus does not mince words but lets every person know that they will all pass through the doorway called death. It will either spell judgment or life based on their repentance.

"...likewise perish..."
It seems to clearly be Jesus' point to stress the certainty of death. However, it could also be that Jesus was forecasting what type of death the Jews would experience at the hands of the Romans in A.D. 70. Having rejected their Messiah, God would render justice upon them. The implication or double meaning tucked within this passage suggests the depth of Jesus' teaching and nature of prophetic material. It could have multiple fulfillments.

"Do you suppose that those on whom the tower in Siloam fell and killed them, were worse culprits than all the men who lived in Jerusalem?"
In order to strengthen Jesus' case, he drew upon another local tragedy: the falling of the tower of Siloam in which eighteen people died. There is no record of this incident outside of the biblical record, so one is left to draw clues only from here. There was a tower in Siloam -- most likely an aqueduct tower carrying water across the countryside to the cities -- which collapsed and killed eighteen people who happened to be gathered around it. Because of the large number of people who perished, it is assumed that these were workmen working under it or that this particular tower was in the marketplace where a large number of people could assemble around it. What is obvious from Jesus' statement was that those who were killed by the tower were considered

innocent of any transgression involving the tower. These were innocent people, not fleeing bank robbers or rapists.

The Jewish mind could not rest with this type of controversy and sought to avoid the actual implications of "innocent" people dying, and so they chose to believe that God caused this tower to fall on these people because they had committed some great sin. They had to have been greater sinners than everyone else or God would not have allowed this tower to fall on them.

"I tell you, no..."
Jesus attacks this arrogant theory and does not allow the people to escape the fact that these people died because they were not "innocent." In fact, there are no "innocent" people in this world, but all are under the condemnation of sin and deserve to die. All have a death sentence hanging over their heads which could be executed at any moment.

Imagine the white-hot emotion of Jesus as He saw these peoples' minds bending upon the impact of this tragedy to support and, in fact, enhance their own self-righteous arrogance rather than as something designed to humble them before a Holy God. They were able to conclude from God's justice displayed right in front of them that they remained alive, not because of His grace but because of their own righteousness. It was this incredible arrogance and pride that activated the words, "I TELL YOU, NO"!

"...but, unless you repent..."

Jesus hammered the point home that they must repent or remain under the sentence of death rightly handed down by God Almighty. They must change the way they think. It is a small wonder that Jesus did not execute them right on the spot for their vile arrogance, but His gracious patience and forbearance allowed Him to hand out mercy and peace to those whose very thoughts blasphemed His Father.

"...you will all likewise perish."

Jesus' point was clearly still the certainty of everyone's death. However, it can also be suggested that the word *likewise* could mean that Jesus was saying something very specific to His listeners that day. They were to perish as swiftly at the hands of the Romans as those eighteen who fell under the tower in Siloam. There was no mercy, only quick and sudden destruction. The power of the Roman legions came and crushed the Jews swiftly and brought about the destruction of their nation. Their cities lay in ruins.

"And He began telling this parable:"

Jesus punctuated His address with a story about the favored fig tree. In this parable He declared that Israel's favored position in God's eyes would come to an end (at least for a period) because of a lack of fruitfulness.

Delighting in Jesus

Live in the light of life's fragility. Jesus' words cut through our foggy thinking about our life. We should be grateful for every day! We should live every day as if it were our last.

What words of love do you need to say to your family and friends in case you don't get another day? What would you make sure you do if this was your last day? Let's take a look at the truths of this hard parable.

Tragedy happens because of sin. Our whole lives are under the sentence of death because of our rebellion and selfishness. Jesus, our Sin Bearer, becomes more precious when you understand how precarious our lives are each day. We need to seek grace every day to break through our own default settings of sin and selfishness. Thank Jesus that our sentence of death falls on Him. Thank Jesus for the wisdom He wants to give you today. Take delight in the Savior who wants you, loves you, and died for you.

What is interesting about Jesus' statement is the harsh nature of reality that He forces people to examine. *Everybody is a sinner. Everybody is going to die.* It is amazing that God is willing to deal with us at all. Jesus doesn't coddle people. In fact, He looks to wake people up to the reality of the world around them. This is Jesus using the first of the pieces of God's armor—truth. When we develop "nice" theories about death or rosy reasons why we are not as bad as other people, we allow the enemy to lie to us. The gospels record the truth about life, death, and tragedy; and truth's bracing slap wakes us up to living every day and drawing in God's gift of forgiveness.

Chapter 8
Jesus Teaches on Prayer - Part I

Key Verses

Luke 11:1-13 - *And it came about that while He was praying in a certain place, after He had finished, one of His disciples said to Him, "Lord teach us to pray just as John also taught his disciples." And He said to them, "When you pray, say: 'Father, hallowed be Thy name. Thy kingdom come. Give us each day our daily bread. And forgive us our sins, For we ourselves also forgive everyone who is indebted to us. And lead us not into temptation.'" And He said to them, "Suppose one of you shall have a friend, and shall go to him at midnight, and say to him, 'Friend, lend me three loaves; for a friend of mine has come to me from a journey, and I have nothing to set before Him'; and from inside he shall answer and say, 'Do not bother me; the door has already been shut and my children and I are in bed; I cannot get up and give you anything.' I tell you, even though he will not get up and give him anything because he is his friend, yet because of his persistence he will get up and give him as much as he needs. "And I say to you, ask, and it shall be given to you; seek, and you shall find; knock, and it shall be opened to you. For everyone who asks, receives; and he who seeks, finds; and to him who knocks, it shall be opened. Now suppose one of you fathers is asked by his son for a fish; he will not give him a snake instead of a fish, will he? Or if he is asked for an egg, he will not give him a scorpion, will he? If you then, being evil, know how to give good gifts to your children, how much more shall your heavenly Father give the Holy Spirit to those who ask Him?"*

The Story Detailed

The Setting

To really understand the tension and mystery of this lesson on prayer, one must understand three crucial background elements: the teaching that took place during this time, the location where this episode took place, and the timing of the episode.

The Teaching

This particular parable is set in what has been called the *center section of Luke*. It is usually defined as the Perean ministry. In this section, which is only relayed in Luke's gospel, Jesus relates thirteen parables of immense value.

1. The Good Samaritan
   10:25-37

2. The Unexpected House Guest
   11:5-13

3. The Foolish Rich Man
   12:13-21

Jesus Teaches on Prayer - Part 1

4. The Barren Fig Tree
   13:1-9

5. The Great Supper
   14:16-24

6. The Lost Sheep
   15:4-7

7. The Lost Coin
   15:8-10

8. The Lost Son
   15:11-32

9. The Unjust Steward
   16:1-8

10. The Rich Man and Lazarus
    16:19-31

11. The Unrighteous Judge
    18:1-8

12. The Pharisee and the Publican
    18:9-14

Although it is possible to divide up the parables in a different manner, these are generally the agreed-upon parables of the center section of Luke. This material is invaluable as it shows us Jesus' heart. The teaching and depth of emotion in these stories reveal facets of the Savior that we cannot bear to miss.

Place

One of the difficulties of this center section of Luke is that there are no city names like there were in Jesus' Galilean ministry. This makes it impossible to trace Jesus' movements in detail. However, the details that are available have created quite a controversy. There are three verses in this very large section that identify places where Jesus was during this Perean ministry - Luke 9:51, 13:22, and 17:11.

- Luke 9:51 - *When the days were approaching for His ascension, He was determined to go Jerusalem.*

From this verse it is clear that Jesus was going south out of Galilee where most of His ministry took place.

- Luke 13:22 - *And He was passing through from one city and village to another, teaching, and proceeding on His way to Jerusalem.*

Again this passage mentions that He was moving toward Jerusalem. There was an abandonment of the northern sections of Palestine and a continued movement south.

Jesus Teaches on Prayer - Part 1

- Luke 17:11 - *And it came about while He was on the way to Jerusalem, that He was passing between Samaria and Galilee.*

This verse thrusts us back north and further away from Jerusalem. This has caused untold difficulties for numerous commentators. Some have even abandoned the veracity of Scripture on this one verse. This is hasty, however, as three potential harmonization's have presented themselves.

First, there are those who believe that these three passages describe three separate trips that Jesus made from north to south during the last six months of His ministry. Second, there is a group of scholars who harmonize this problem by saying we are not given enough details to know what really took place. And third, there is a group of scholars that believe that this refers to one and the same journey toward Jerusalem but does not refer to the events in chronological order. In this explanation, it assumes that Luke arranges the material in this center section topically, not chronologically. This final solution seems to be the most reasonable.

Also, in this particular episode the place is not referred to specifically except as "a certain place." It is assumed that this is somewhere in the Perean countryside. Since Jesus made frequent trips into this region during His last six months of ministry and since John did the bulk of his ministry in this region as well, it is safe to assume that this was where Jesus and the disciples were when the question "teach us to pray" arose. It is possible that John was brought up because of the preponderance of references to Him by His former disciples when they traveled past areas where He traveled with them.

Perea is referred to as the land beyond the Jordan. When the Pharisees hounded Jesus after the raising of Lazarus, He went into Perea. Prior to this He ministered there on His last journey toward Jerusalem.

Time

When Jesus began His journey south out of Galilee and towards Jerusalem, He knew that He would have to pay for the sins of the whole world on a cross at Jerusalem. He had between six and nine months left to live to train His disciples. He had to fully inculcate all He wanted them to know within the next six-month period. He knew the date of His death— Passover -- for He knew He had to present Himself as King one last time on the fulfillment date of Daniel's prophecy (9:27). He knew that He would be rejected and that six days later He would become the Passover Lamb for everyone.

The Request

As one begins to examine this section on prayer, it is important to stop and consider in detail a few items before the meat of the discussion begins.

The Disciple

The disciple who asked this question was clearly the representative of a group of disciples who wanted Jesus to teach them to pray. He betrayed his representative status with the "us" reference in his question.

We cannot assume that this was one of the twelve apostles. In fact, it is best to assume that it was not one of them but rather one of the seventy disciples who had just returned from their first preaching tour (Luke 10:17-20) and wanted further instruction. They had seen the miracles the Lord had given them the power to do. They had preached and had been aware of the responsiveness of people. They sensed something was missing though, and they were beginning to understand what it was. They felt it every time Jesus prayed. There was an intimacy and fellowship with the Father in His prayers that they had never heard before. They were excited about the service that they had performed for Jesus and the Father, however, Jesus kept introducing this new element into the equation. There was something more significant than service for God—a personal relationship with Him. Jesus said it in Luke 10:20 and they heard it every time they had the privilege to overhear His prayers.

A slight inclination of the motive for the question entered into the disciple's statement: "as John taught his disciples." Some of Jesus' disciples had formerly been John's disciples and most likely related the lessons that they were taught at the feet of Jesus' forerunner, John. The other disciples longed for this same intimate formal training in spiritual matters that John's disciples had received.

The Question

With the finality of this journey in mind, it is amazing to realize that Jesus had waited until that time to teach His disciples to pray, and then that it was their question which prompted the lesson. There is a great truth here about when to engage in teaching: teach them when the pupil is ready and not before even if you know that they will desperately need the material later. Too often in our churches we are teaching material that the congregation is not wanting. The powerful truths then fall on deaf ears. Jesus was the master at getting His disciples to want to hear after seeing Him model a practice or truth.

Teach

The word that the disciple used in asking Jesus is a present tense word and can carry two separate ideas: "teach us to be praying" and "teach us how to pray." Great controversy has arisen over which one of these the disciple was after. It seems best to realize that Jesus' answer encompassed both ways of interpreting the question. Let's spend some time thinking through each question.

"Teach us how to pray"

This question is clearly within the disciple's request as Jesus deals with this topic first. It is doubtful that the disciple was saying, "Teach me a rote prayer that I can use and say all the time the same way." This would be ridiculous in light of the motivation for the question. It is, therefore, doubtful that Jesus answered the question with rote prayer. He told them how to pray in the broader, more general arenas of attitude, intent, and types of petition.

"Teach us to be praying"

The disciple seemed to be asking Jesus to say something that will glue the need for prayer permanently into their minds and make them pray. Most often this is done in preaching by putting people on a guilt trip for not praying. This particular method seems to fail every time. The greatest prayer warriors to have ever graced the Christian scene (men and women who were literally always praying) tell us that they still felt guilty about not praying enough—men like E.M. Bounds, C.H. Spurgeon, and Billy Graham. What is it that Jesus could say that would so rivet the disciples to prayer that they could not help but pray?

Jesus did not take the ineffective guilt-trip route when answering this part of the disciple's question. The wonderfully powerful story Jesus told accomplished the disciples' desire of permanent motivation to keep on praying.

John Taught

This is one of the few glimpses we have of John's ministry other than baptism. He obviously took responsibility for the complete spiritual development of those who were following Him. His legacy of direct instructional periods with the inner core carried His name and purpose past the point of His death. This small-group topical instruction on the basics of spirituality is essential for permanent infection with real Christianity.

It is also possible that those disciples who had previously been John's disciples were constantly mentioning what John had taught them. This would be heightened by the return to the places where John's ministry had taken place. It is not beyond possibility that the natural rivalry between disciples brought this question to the forefront as the newer disciples sought to "one up" those older disciples (now apostles) who had been with John: "You were trained by John; we were trained by Jesus!" Jesus used what may have been prompted by petty rivalry to teach important truth. Jesus is the master teacher looking for the opportune moments to drop truth to the core of our being.

The Lord's Prayer?

This section has often been called the Lord's Prayer and is referred to by many people this way. This, however, is not the case - It's the Disciple's Prayer. There is no evidence that Jesus prayed this prayer. The only long recorded prayer of Jesus is in John 17, which should really bear the title the Lord's Prayer.

Relation to the Matthew Passage

Much has been written about how this Lukan passage is textually different from the Matthew passage. This controversy has led many to spiritual shipwreck as they falsely assume the two passages must be the same. The following is a summary of the differences between the two texts. The additional Matthew material is in capital letters.

Jesus Teaches on Prayer - Part 1

> *OUR Father, WHO ART IN HEAVEN,*
> *Hallowed be Thy Name.*
> *Thy kingdom come,*
> *THY WILL BE DONE*
> *ON EARTH AS IT IS IN HEAVEN.*
> *Give us this day our daily bread,*
> *And forgive us our debts, AS we also have forgiven our debtors.*
> *And do not lead us into temptation, BUT DELIVER US FROM EVIL. FOR THINE IS THE KINGDOM, AND THE POWER, AND THE GLORY FOREVER.*
> *AMEN.*

It is clear that substantial material is added in the Matthew account. This caused such a great stir in the early centuries of the church that a scribe added the additional material to Luke so that they would be the same. It is, however, unnecessary to make the two accounts agree exactly (unless one is arguing that this is the formula of prayer or that Jesus never said anything more than once). It is clear that the sermon Jesus preached in Matthew is in a totally different place and time than when He instructed a small band of eager disciples in Luke. Jesus does not have to use the exact same words for it was not His intent to start a ritualistic prayer. As an itinerant evangelist, Jesus probably said many things more than once and used different settings for the same sayings. It is only in a western culture obsessed with copyrights and exact correspondence that this is even a problem.

Jesus obviously felt free to amend His own teaching to reflect the point He was seeking to make at that particular time. He was seeking to implant a general pattern of prayer in His disciples and not get them to memorize a specific prayer. The general pattern is to deal with God's desires before one deals with his own desires. The petitions are topically as follows:

- First petition: Honor God
- Second petition: God's rulership
- Third petition: Personal needs
- Fourth petition: Forgiveness
- Fifth petition: Freedom from potential spiritual bondage

It is not the desire of this writer, nor is it possible to explore all the depth and treasures that have been buried deep in this section called the Lord's Prayer. Our purpose is to explore it to a sufficient depth to understand the main purpose the Lord uttered it. Many fine works on this subject abound and in far more depth. The eager student might want to consult them. Thomas Watson's *The Lord's Prayer* is a good starting place.

Jesus' Three-Part Teaching

The Pharisees also taught their disciples to pray and paid attention to incredible detail in their teaching. They ascribed incredible importance to miniscule things like the exact position of the body, the degrees of inclination of the torso when kneeling, and other trivialities. The ridiculous minutia to which the Pharisees instructed on prayer contrasted completely with the wonderful simplicity that Jesus teaches.

He only wanted to get across three points:

1. **What to say...**

    Jesus' first response to the disciple's question was to answer how to pray with only one seeming reference to the motivation to pray. He outlined the way His disciples should pray. It has been suggested that when Jesus says, "When you pray, say..." it was His way of giving the disciples the exact formula to pray to the Father. This exact wording would violate the principle of non-repetitive prayer that He outlined in Matthew 6. Matthew's discussion of this particular prayer formula says that Jesus said to pray "in this way." The freshness, spontaneity, and intimate relationship are lost if this prayer of Jesus is made into a rote prayer. It would be a shame to lose part of what the disciples were after in order to support a system built on one word of the text.

2. **When to say it...**

    Jesus stated that the disciples who asked this question were already praying, and He assumed that they would keep on praying. He says, "when you pray." His goal was to alter certain key elements of their prayer lives.

3. **Who to say it to—the Father.**

    Jesus continued to shock the disciples with His suggestions and this case was no exception. But this was just the shock the disciples were hoping for. Never before had a Jew been permitted to address the Holy and Righteous God as his own Father. It smacked of familiarity and irreverence. It suggested that one had forgotten that he was a sinner in need of redemption and mercy from God Almighty. One hears these clarion calls again in our day that the easy familiarity with which Christians are taught to pray has led to a diminishing of the majesty and sovereignty that God is thought to possess. Jesus did not share this sentiment and offered His disciples an intimate relationship. Jesus enjoyed a special relationship with God the Father and suggested that His disciples enter into that relationship through Him. It is intimacy of relationship with the living and awesome God that leads to praise and righteous living.

One must not forget that there is a reverence with this address that is not in any way irreverent or disrespectful. It is relationally oriented without being degrading or demeaning.

First Petition: Hallowed Be Thy Name

The word *hallowed* means "to make holy, to separate, to magnify, exalt." This suggests that Jesus thought the first thing needed to be done was to contemplate the majesty and wonder of God with the petition that it be raised even higher and treated with more respect the world over. The whole of Jesus' ministry and life began and ended with the majesty and sovereignty of God the Father.

An honest petitioner who seriously contemplates this first petition and prays it would be unable to continue in a lifestyle that involved cussing, profanity, and blasphemy.

Kenneth Wuest, in his book, *Word Studies from the Greek New Testament*, renders this petition: "Father, cause Your Name to be set apart as sacred and the object of veneration."[1] This gives the gist of the tenses and words in the original language.

Second Petition: Thy Kingdom Come

This second petition is the cause of much concern by commentators because of their differing views of the millennial kingdom. There are some who understand that Jesus meant only to establish a spiritual kingdom: others who believe that Jesus meant to establish an earthly political kingdom in the future; and still others who understand that He came to do both. It is best to see that both purposes were in Jesus' mind when He uttered this petition, especially in the light of the Scriptures that refer to His kingship over us spiritually, and the Scriptures that refer to His return to establish a political kingdom in Jerusalem.

The kingdom of God means the rule of God over every aspect of life -- individually, family, governmentally, and internationally. God seeks to rule over the individual and enlist him in a bigger purpose than his or her own pleasures to make him an agent of the kingdom of light rather than the kingdom of darkness ascribing to its rules and customs.

God seeks to establish His rule over a family and have it carry out His dictates and organizational structure. God has plans for Christian families. They are to participate fully in the present form of the kingdom of God.

God seeks to rule over societies and establish His laws and morality codes to better any nation that will adopt His rule. Our country was built upon the bedrock of the morality of the laws of God, and we have seen the country disintegrate from within as we have trampled over the fences that God's law provides. We make a grave mistake if we believe that we should not take every opportunity to establish the rule of God's law in the society in which we live. Just because we know that we will not be ultimately successful until Jesus comes back doesn't mean that we should not seek the establishment of the rule of God in the county, state, and country where we live. It is incredibly illogical.

God seeks to establish His rule over nations and over the entire planet. This will not take place until Jesus Christ comes again to rule and reign and put down the final satanic rebellion against God's rule.

Come

It is the Lord's desire to see all these aspects of the kingdom come. We are to pray diligently that God the Father would bring it about. This prayer obviously involves a willingness on your part to allow God to be absolute Lord of your life and your family life. It involves surrendering and petitioning God regarding the future. This particular petition has incredible direct implications on the lethargic Christian who has been running his or her life on their own.

Third Petition: Give Us This Day Our Daily Bread

This is a fairly straightforward petition aimed at keeping the petitioner alive. Jesus does not ignore the needs of the body, even though he does put its needs after the greater desire for the heart of God. It is instructive that one should first determine the number one desire of God before one moves on to petition for the needs of oneself.

The word *daily* is an interesting word and can be more literally translated "needed bread." The word has taken on the idea of daily because in that day bread was the main staple and would constitute the substance of the main meal. Therefore the needed bread became the daily bread. Whole-grain bread constituted the major part of most meals. This whole grain was formed into a circle and allowed to rise a little and then baked. This round loaf was what kept you alive each day.

There is also, in this petition for daily bread, the hint that there are other types of bread than just physical bread. Jesus Himself is the bread of life with the major emphasis being about the spiritual need people have to be connected to God. Realize that when you are praying for your daily bread, you are also praying for your relational needs to be met, your monetary needs, and your significance needs. All of the things that go into making you a healthy, growing person are wrapped up in this petition.

Fourth Petition: Forgive Us Our Sins

This petition is the only conditional clause in the whole prayer. The way that Jesus speaks of bitterness is clear that God never designed our systems to handle it.

This clause links forgiveness granted to us on the basis of our forgiving others. It says that if we do not forgive others, then we do not want God to forgive us of our sins. The questions that immediately come to mind are: How could this linkage take place? How could the forgiveness which is freely offered in Christ be linked to the individual believer's forgiveness of others?

A number of explanations have been offered: but the best one would suggest that the forgiveness of Christ is stored in your name when you accept Christ, and you can experience it when you ask for forgiveness. That is unless you have harbored grudges and animosity toward others. It is impossible for you to comprehend, receive, and enjoy the forgiveness in Christ with bitterness in your person. It would be the same as if someone put a huge inheritance in your name but put conditions upon your withdrawal of the money.

To overcome bitterness, let's examine the Scriptures:

> 1. Examine the offense and realize that it was without intent or the full intent that it accomplished. (Luke 23:34)
>
> 2. Christ's forgiveness of our debt to Him is huge. How is it possible for you to hold another

responsible to the point of injury when you have been forgiven so much? (Matthew 18:21)

3. Ask yourself how this can work out for the greater progress of your individual conformity to Christ? (Romans 8:28) It is only when the benefits for the offense are greater than the supposed evil that we will be able to rejoice that it happened to us.

4. Realize that without forgiveness we are without the mercy and lovingkindness of God. (Matthew 6:14,16)

5. Realize that their offense might be our opportunity to suffer for their ultimate salvation. (1 Peter 2:21-25)

6. Justice must still be served and if you did wrong, then you must bear the penalty. (1 Peter 2: 18-20)

7. Pray for the person you're bitter toward and the bitterness will soon diminish. (Matthew 5:44)

Fifth Petition: Lead Us Not Into Temptation

This is an extremely delicate interpretation that can lead to blasphemy if it is not examined in light of the whole counsel of the Word of God.

James says that it is impossible for God to tempt anyone and He cannot be tempted to do evil Himself. Therefore it is impossible for God to be the direct agent by which we are led into a temptation where we may sin and fall. It is not necessary to pray for God to not do what He isn't capable of doing. We must look in another direction to understand this petition.

The word *temptation* can be translated in two different ways. One way is to translate it as *temptation* or "the lure to do evil." The second way is translate it as *trials or problems or testing*, which every person wants to avoid, but which God uses to move us toward the image of Christ when we don't grow in other ways. If the word in this verse is translated trials, then Jesus is suggesting that a believer's petition to the Father is to not send them into trials or problems that might accomplish His will or might be as a result of their own stupid decisions. This is consistent with Jesus' request in the garden that if there were some other way to accomplish the salvation of mankind other than the cross, He would have preferred the Father to take it. He clearly did not want to go through the trial He was about to experience. It is therefore assumed that we can petition the Father to be excused from trials and problems. Is there another alternative? Another way of seeing this interpretation is to understand that the Lord is suggesting that many of the problems believers would encounter are because of their own foolish choices, and He could be suggesting that they ask the Father to "forgive" their choices and eliminate the earned trial.

Another way of understanding the problem of this petition is to explore the word *lead*. This alternative would see that the believer is being told by the Lord to petition the Father to remove them from any pathway that will lead them by a temptation that is too big for them to handle. It is a prayer to accomplish 1 Corinthians 10:13, *Show me the way to escape the pathways to temptation.* It is consistent to ask God to move us away from temptation and use His infinite knowledge of the future to rescue the struggling believer from danger of which he is not aware. This interpretation seems to carry with it tacit approval for God to do whatever He has to do to remove the disciples from harm's way.

Delighting in Jesus

Spend some time interacting with God about the five basic topics that He says are crucial for a healthy spiritual life. Look at each topic and begin talking with God about it.

First petition: Honor God

Lord, I need to honor you for all that you have done for me and will do for me. I want to honor you for your attributes, your nature, and your names. I want to be grateful for all that you have done for me...

Second petition: God's rulership

God, I want your kingdom and your ways to be used more in my life and in my community. I am sorry that I am not living more clearly for you. I am hopeful that your kingdom will break into my world and straighten things out. I also pray that you would return and set up your actual kingdom here on earth...

Third petition: Personal needs

Lord, I do ask you to supply for all the various personal and relational needs that I have in my life. I thank you for what you have done in the past. Please keep supplying. Also, give me eyes to see and ears to hear the various ways that you are meeting my needs…

Fourth petition: Forgiveness

Lord, I need to forgive others, specifically _____. I am struggling with what they did to me but want to release any vengeance to you. I want your ways to be my ways. You were willing to endure all kinds of abuse to accomplish the goal of saving the world. Help me remember you… I have committed many trespass sins and I want you to forgive me, so I must forgive others for their sins against me.

Fifth petition: Freedom from potential spiritual bondage

Lord, the Devil is constantly trying to derail my life and potential. Keep me in your loving embrace and swat away the destructive temptations that come from the enemy. Right now these are the temptations and tests that I am struggling with…

With Jesus as your guide, you should be able to spend at least five minutes talking with God about each of these different topics. Talk to God about each of these areas. Allow Him to direct you and encourage you about these various issues. Each time you approach God with these topics the discussion will change, and you will be changed by the discussion.

In the next chapter we discuss Part 2 on the subject of prayer, and we will examine the Lord's comments on the three remaining subjects:

- Why should we pray?
- What should be our motivation?
- What should we expect when we pray?

The Lord's exciting comments on these extremely relevant issues will grip you with new desire to pray.

Chapter 9
Jesus Teaches on Prayer - Part 2

Key Verses

Luke 11:5-13 - *And He said to them, "Suppose one of you shall have a friend, and shall go to him at midnight, and say to him, 'friend, lend me three loaves; for a friend of mine has come to me from a journey, and I have nothing to set before Him'; and from inside he shall answer and say, 'Do not bother me; the door has already been shut and my children and I are in bed; I cannot get up and give you anything.' "I tell you, even though he will not get up and give him anything because he is his friend, yet because of his persistence he will get up and give him as much as he needs. "And I say to you, ask, and it shall be given to you; seek, and you shall find; knock, and it shall be opened to you. "For everyone who asks, receives; and he who seeks, finds; and to him who knocks, it shall be opened. "Now suppose one of you fathers is asked by his son for a fish; he will not give him a snake instead of a fish, will he? "Or if he is asked for an egg, he will not give him a scorpion, will he? "If you then, being evil, know how to give good gifts to your children, how much more shall your heavenly Father give the Holy Spirit to those who ask Him?"*

The Story Detailed

After modeling prayer for the disciples, Jesus proceeded to other matters involving prayer. He dealt with *why* we should pray and *what we should expect* when we pray. All this to answer the disciples' request, "Teach us to pray." There was a hidden desire within this request for Jesus to tell them something about prayer so profound that they would be compelled to pray -- something which would make them want to pray and make it impossible not to pray. He addressed this unspoken request in a second section of His impromptu seminars on prayer. When rightly understood, Jesus accomplished His goal and created a desire for prayer within the disciples that would not go away.

Why should we pray?
Jesus tells the disciples a story to bring them within reach of the greatest truth about prayer. It is fascinating to observe how Jesus used stories to make His points. He understood that a key truth contextualized in a story would be remembered much longer than just rote facts. The story of the friend at midnight reverberates through the hallways of our minds, seeking to teach us essential truths about prayer. If we pay special attention, we can uncover the key motivation (the why) behind prayer.

Hospitality
The story of the friend at midnight seems strange to modern ears because of the cultural differences regarding hospitality. In the Near Eastern culture where travel was not common

and towns and villages were few and far between, hospitality was essential. There weren't Holiday Inns or McDonald's dotting the terrain to stay the night or get a hot meal. The traveler depended upon the hospitality of others for life. It was considered a moral outrage to deny someone hospitality. Because of the marauding bands of robbers and thieves, one could be signing a death warrant for a refused traveler. Plus, one never knew when they might be the lonely traveler who needed someone's hospitality. The International Standard Bible Encyclopedia explains that the received traveler is made the literal master of the house during his stay. The host will perform for him the most servile duties and will not even sit at a meal with his guest unless he is specifically requested to do so.

The following expectations were what placed the friend at midnight under such a burden to get the bread:

1. It was considered morally outrageous to refuse to be hospitable (i.e., it was akin to potentially giving the traveler a death sentence).

2. If one did not respond with hospitality, he could not expect the hospitality of others if he was in need while traveling.

3. There were marauding bands of robbers and thieves that took advantage of people on the road or in the open after dark. (Genesis 18, Judges 19, Luke 10)

4. There were few, if any, provisions for travelers like there are today. There were no restaurants or motels. There were some inns to stay at but these were few,

small, and often filled; plus they were typically centers for evil doings.

The Need

From what has been stated above, the person was in desperate need to find something to set before his hungry houseguest. Jesus seemed to be saying that truly effective prayer springs from a need. Some have suggested from this story that the need is someone else's. But an understanding of the culture would intimate that the person doing the asking was as interested in meeting his own need as his friend's. One can accurately say that without a felt need, no real effective prayer takes place. In order to pray effectively, one must have a need and feel it. If we feel we need nothing, then we ask God for nothing (Revelation 3:20).

The House

We find Jesus' order of persistence to be somewhat askew -- ask, seek, and knock. Within our culture it would be seek, knock, and ask. We can only make sense of this if we understand the houses of that period.

The typical house in a Near Eastern village had two inner rooms in the back of the house with windows, a central living room with a door and bolt, and a courtyard with another door and bolt. It is most likely that the person in need went to the window of his friend's bedroom and asked him to give him bread. He received a negative response, but he refused to take "no" for an answer. The man in Jesus' story says that unbolting the door would awaken the children and the rest of the house, so he would not grant the man's request.

As has been shown, there were probably two bolted doors to contend with. In the pitch black of midnight under a moonless sky he sought out the door of the courtyard. Having inched his way along the wall of the man's house, he found the door to the courtyard that was bolted from the inside. When he found the door, he began to knock to awaken his friend and let him know that he would not take "no" for an answer. The knocking on the courtyard door -- being across the distance of the house -- could be ignored at first. But as the man continued knocking, it became louder and louder and he was obviously not going away. The man's friend inside aroused himself and unbolted the door of the living room, waking up the children. He made his way across the courtyard, unbolted that door, and let the man in, giving him the bread he desired.

The Door Bolt

The door bolt of the Near Eastern home would be very noisy and cumbersome. As described above, there were probably two of them -- one on the living room door and one on the courtyard door. There were vertical bars on the door that a large wooden plank or metal rod was inserted into horizontally which would keep the door from being opened from the outside. In many countries these types of door bolts are employed even today to keep the residences safe at night. Often more than one horizontal rod is used to secure the door. Once a person was inside this system, it was very involved to let someone in.

Jesus' Three-Part Commentary

Having told the story of the friend at midnight, Jesus gave a three-part commentary so that His disciples would not miss the crucial application points. They were destined to remember the story, but it was the lesson behind it that He wanted them to take home. Now that Jesus had their attention, He explained what He meant.

Part 1

Persistence

The NASB translates Jesus' point: "Yet because of his *persistence* he will get up and give him as much as he needs." The word *persistence* carries only half the power of the word *anaideian*, which appears this one time in the New Testament. The word also carries the sense of *shamelessness*. The person doing the requesting felt the need so desperately that he was not only persistent but also shameless in making the request. All the normal social customs were discarded because of the immense need. There was no proper decorum to his persistent request. The KJV translates the word *importunity*, which is a closer translation but still misses the power of both halves of the meaning. *Shameless persistence* seems the best way to translate this word.

Jesus' point is that shameless persistence with the sovereign God of the universe wins the day. We see precedence for this point in the Scriptures as Abraham was shamelessly persistent in pleading for Sodom and the five cities of the plain. Moses was shamelessly persistent in pleading for the nation of Israel. The Syro-phoenecian woman was shamelessly persistent in seeking healing for her boy. Hannah was shamelessly persistent in seeking to have her infertility changed so she could bear a child. All of these and others -- who were shamelessly persistent -- received what they asked for.

The stumbling block within this parable and this particular point, however, is that it makes our sovereign, loving, good, gracious, and all-powerful God appear as a grudging Scrooge dividing out blessings only when He is pestered to death. Since this is clearly not who God is, commentators reinterpret the point of this parable to put God in a more favorable light. However, as admirable as this imaginative interpretation is, it hides a crucial truth about prayer. *Shameless persistence wins the day.* It is effective. Jesus believes this point so much that He says it again in an even harsher story in Luke 18:1 -- the story of the unjust judge. Jesus is not teaching about who God is; He is teaching about how to pray effectively. We must take Jesus at His word and not let our own mental connections cloud the truth of effective prayer. Don't let the truth of prayer bleed into your understanding of the nature of God when He has clearly explained and demonstrated who He is in other places. There are many mysteries in prayer, and we would do best to leave them in God's hands and keep praying the way He taught us.

As much as he needs
Jesus states that the person who is shamelessly persistent not only receives what he wants but as much as he needs. The person with the hospitality problem got more than just three loaves. The implication is obvious—once the request is going to be granted, the well keeps on giving until the need is

erased. The friend who was finally aroused was willing to give the petitioner whatever he needed at that point.

Part 2

Jesus wanted to make a further point involving this story and the principles of successful prayer. He introduced this new but connected truth with the phrase, "And I say unto you..." This lets us know that what Jesus is about to say is connected to the story and the point He just made, but it involves a new point as well.

Ask

The emphasis in this second section of Jesus' commentary is on the verbs *ask, seek, and knock*. The first is *ask*. The word is in the present tense and would be more accurately translated *ask and continue asking* and it shall be given unto you. The word is used only for the asking by an inferior to a superior. This is the way Jesus always suggested that His disciples address the Father. An interesting note is that Jesus used a different word for Himself to make a request from the Father -- a word that denotes an equal requesting from another equal. Jesus is clearly saying that without asking, nothing is received. *One must ask.*

The radical motivating idea that Jesus interjects into our thinking on prayer is that asking gets an answer. Jesus sought to motivate His disciples (and us) to pray by letting them know that if they asked on a consistent basis, then they would receive. It is radical. There are no conditions -- just asking.

(This gives us motivation to pray because it will be successful.)

It has been suggested that Jesus often stated principles of life that were broadly applicable throughout life and related them to our relationship with God. This seems to be true here. It is a general principle that those who ask and keep on asking receive what they ask for. This particular truth has propelled many to monetary, vocational, and marital success. Jesus is applying it to the arena of intimacy with God. It works everywhere.

It has also been suggested that Jesus' three-fold division -- ask, seek, and knock -- are levels in the prayer experience. This definitely fits with the story He told. There are certain requests that need only asking to receive an answer. There are others that require seeking to receive an answer; and there are still other requests that require persistent, shameless knocking to receive the answer. This is a valid conclusion from the story, but one must keep in mind that the point of all three levels is that the requester receives what he or she is after. They do not stop asking until they receive what they requested. One goes on to seeking if simple continuous asking does not receive the request and so on through knocking.

Seek

The word *seek* is also in the present tense and connotes the continuous seeking of the desired benefit. The word seek is *ziteite* and means *active endeavoring* to obtain the fulfillment of his needs. There are three potential directions that this seeking points to in your relationship with God.

1. There is a hint in this word that the answer is already present but must be found. That is, the persistent asking of the previous stage has produced an answer but requires you to become involved in seeking the answer. God has provided it, but you must find it. It is often true that the gifts God gives in answer to our prayer are ignored because we thought or hoped the answer would come in some other form (like the man who prays for money and is offered a job, or the woman who prays for a husband and yet rejects the friendship of a godly man because he is not what she expected).

2. Another direction this word can take in the prayer is asking when the petitioner has not yet really apprehended God. This carries with it the idea that one is asking but not really, surely, or definitely in the presence of God. (There are numerous passages that suggest the believer must seek the Lord diligently and then only with this type of seeking will he be found.) The emphasis here is clearly on the Lord as the object of the search. Seek Him and you will find Him and once you have found Him, then all your wants and needs will be met or transformed.

3. Following the storyline it suggests that the petitioner needs to seek for the doorway through which his desire may be met. In other words, many people pray for something for God to give them, but they pursue it with selfish purposes or immoral reasons. The idea here is that God wants us to keep asking for the desired result to change our motive or way of asking so that he might grant the request to us.

Knock

The idea of knocking in the Near Eastern culture is different from that in the western culture. Our culture knocks to determine if someone is home, assuming that they will answer the door if they are there. The Oriental culture knocks to gain attention and provide entrance. Someone is always home, but the door is so far from where the people are that they need to be alerted to your presence at the door. It is this concept that skews our thinking so much that we are unable to embrace this truth about prayer. Is God a distant deity needing to be roused from sleep by our constant banging on His door? The answer is clearly no! Then why tell us to knock until someone answers? Remember that the person who was knocking always received what he requested once he was acknowledged as being there by the opening of the door. It is entirely possible that Jesus is saying we should keep on knocking until we receive what we are knocking for. Other than this idea, we are left to wonder at the mystery of prayer that requires our shameless persistence towards a God who sincerely desires to meet our needs and has all the power capable to accomplish it.

Some have thought that knocking means asking with action and wishing for opportunity. This knocking at the door of opportunity is not suggested by Jesus' story and should therefore be discarded.

The clear teaching of Jesus is this: *one should come to God with rising intensity and persistence until he receives what he needs.*

Part 3

Jesus repeated the idea He had just presented with a new emphasis upon the results. In this section Jesus clearly stressed receiving, finding, and opening. The results are the crux of this section of the commentary.

Everyone

Jesus started this third part of the commentary of the story of the friend at midnight with the first all-inclusive term *everyone who...* This is significant because it clearly extends beyond the disciples who were present at the time to everyone. It also extends beyond the realm of just those who are believers. Anyone who continues to ask receives, anyone who keeps on seeking shall find, and anyone who continues knocking will have the door opened to them. This all-inclusive language -- along with the next story in Jesus' seminar -- suggests that the object of prayer should be God. If anyone continues asking to get to know God, he shall receive that intimate knowledge. If anyone diligently keeps seeking to find God, he shall find God. If anyone keeps banging on the door of heaven that he might enjoy fellowship with God, God will open the door and let him in. Making God the object of your search fits with Jesus' statement in John 17:3: *"This is the eternal life, that they may know You, the only true God, and Jesus Christ whom you have sent."* All the other blessings bestowed in prayer are a result of finding God who can answer any request. It is often true that we ask, seek, and knock from a source that cannot supply what we are after. The man in need sought out the friend who had the loaves of bread, not just the bread itself!

This principle of prayer and life is applicable to all types of prayer requests. Let them ask, seek, and knock and they shall receive what they are asking for. Persistence in prayer does yield results in all areas. This is Jesus' masterstroke of motivation. There is nothing more motivating than the confident assurance that if we ask, we shall receive. If you can persist in it, then you will receive it. Isn't that an amazing idea?

What to Expect

In this last section of Jesus' seminar on prayer, he answered an unasked question regarding prayer and further motivated that small gathering of disciples to pray at all times.

The Story

As was typical, Jesus began with a story and then moved toward the explanation. This story is for everyone, but it is emotionally compelling to the fathers in the group. Jesus asked a few questions of those who were fathers: "Which one among you would substitute a snake for a fish if your son asked for the fish at the evening meal?" "Which one among you would substitute a scorpion for an egg in your son's dinner?" The obvious answer is that no one would.

Fathers

The most prized possession that a man in Jesus' culture could have was a wise and responsible son. There was more pride in a man's sons than in any other possession he owned. This pride would grip the father to provide anything for the betterment of his son. When Jesus grabbed hold of the chain of father-son pride and jerked it, he had their attention.

Snake/Fish

The fish that the son would request would be the small type of fish made as a relish for the main part of a meal. The clear idea is that the son asked for the father to pass the little fish so that the son can have a more tasty meal. In that type of situation, how many fathers would hand their sons a snake instead? It is assumed that the snake is poisonous as every reference to a snake in Scripture suggests a poisonous quality.

Egg/Scorpion

The egg is another relish-type enhancer of the main meal. These condiments to the meal are what made the average meal different and flavorful. What father, when asked innocently by his son (his pride and joy), would purposely give him something harmful and potentially fatal? In that part of the world scorpion stings can be fatal.

The Point

The point is clearly that fathers don't give their sons harmful or deadly things. When the son asks for something good, the father gives the good thing requested. The point Jesus did not deal with is this: What does a father do when a son asks for something harmful or dangerous?

Jesus says, "If you, being evil, know how to give good gifts to your children, how much more shall your heavenly Father give the Holy Spirit to those who ask Him?" Consistent with the idea of motivating the disciples to pray, Jesus let them know that they had nothing to fear by asking the Father for anything. One of the most distressing things about a Christians' prayers and their searching after God is that they honestly believe that God may wreck their lives if they really let Him have full control. They seem to believe that God would purposely substitute a bad thing for the good thing they requested. There is the common belief that if you pray for a happy life, God will make you miserable by sending you to rural Mongolia as a missionary with no fun at all. Jesus motivated His disciples to pray by letting them know that you can't get a bad deal from God. He only gives good things. You can't go wrong by seeking Him out. He holds pleasures forevermore in His right hand.

Jesus' point is precisely clear—*the most enjoyment and the most blessing come from a life of seeking God and His rewards.*

The Holy Spirit
Jesus' mention of the Holy Spirit has caused all types of differing opinions. However, when read at face value with no preconceived pneumonic scheme, it suggests that every Christian can receive more of the Holy Spirit and that receiving more of Him is the same as all the other things we asked for. It is like the son who asked for a new car and a new jacket. He did not receive either, but he did get enough money to go out and purchase both items with plenty left over.

Jesus' mention of the Holy Spirit suggests that the real object of the searching and the asking and the knocking is the triune God. We may be seeking all sorts of different things from Him, but we must realize that we must find Him to have any hope of attaining the requested items. If our focus is so completely on the item requested and not on the Giver of the item, then we could seek to receive the item by illegitimate means. For example, take the people who desire supernatural knowledge and are so focused on what they are seeking that they are willing to attain that knowledge through false religions and occult practices. Others are seeking monetary success and yet concentrate upon it so much that they are willing to cheat, lie, abuse, and bribe to get it. Christians must realize that they cannot desire the item so much that they are willing to receive it from someone other than God or in some other means than in a God-approved manner.

Delighting in Jesus

Are we asking enough of God? Not according to Jesus' teaching on prayer. God is far more interested in us storming the gates of heaven. We must allow God to take what we ask for and sort through the wrong requests as we put more requests out there. Jesus succeeded in motivating those who grasped the clear message of His teaching. How could we do anything but pray when we know that? Let's review what we learned about prayer.

1. *Shameless persistence is a key element in prayer.* While we like to throw in certain qualifiers that are surely important (the request must be in the will of God; our lives must not be sinful; our address must be respectful), Jesus does not include these in His point. The point is to be persistent about our needs. Persistence in prayer yields results.

2. *We cannot receive anything bad from a God who loves us.* This is an absolutely crucial point that needs to be emphasized over and over again. We must submit our ultimate desires to God, but He will not directly give

us that which is harmful or bad for us. Nor will He substitute what is bad for what is good.

3. *Jesus tells us to ask, seek, and knock.* This small three-sentence key unlocked prayer for me in the past, and I am sure that it will open other miracle doorways in the future. I can remember writing down what I thought would be an ideal life five years in the future in all the categories of my life: spirituality, personal development, marriage, family, work, church, friends, enemies, money, and community. I spent time regularly praying that this future ideal world would become reality as I approached it, and God answered my prayers. In some cases he gave me better than what I asked for or differently than I thought was ideal; but he really did change my life through asking, seeking, and knocking.

We can't lose, so let's pray!

Chapter 10
The Widow's Mites

Key Verses

Mark 12:41-44 - *And He sat down opposite the treasury, and began observing how the multitude were putting money into the treasury; and many rich people were putting in large sums. And a poor widow came and put in two small copper coins, which amount to a cent. And calling His disciples to Him, He said to them, "Truly I say to you, this poor widow put in more than all the contributors to the treasury; for they all put in out of their surplus, but she, out of her poverty, put in all she owned, all she had to live on."*

Luke 21:1-4 - *And He looked up and saw the rich putting their gifts into the treasury. And He saw a certain poor widow putting in two small copper coins. And He said, "Truly I say to you, this poor widow put in more than all of them; for they all out of their surplus put into the offering; but she out of her poverty put in all that she had to live on."*

The Story Detailed

The Setting

Jesus was in the midst of His last full day of ministry when this incident with the widow took place. It was the third day of the Passion Week, and it was to be His last day ministering to the crowds in the temple. It was also to be the last time the Pharisees and Sadducees had to deal with His sharp-tongued attacks. On the next day, Thursday, he celebrated Passover with His disciples according to the Galilean custom. Early Friday morning He prayed in the Garden of Gethsemane and was betrayed by Judas.

This last public day is full of varied kinds of activities. The following is what took place on this third day of the Passion Week:

- The Pharisees and Sadducees questioned Jesus' authority. They questioned paying taxes to Caesar.

- The woes were pronounced against the Pharisees and Sadducees. The poor widow cast her offering.

- The Greeks sought an audience with Jesus.

- Jesus summarized His ministry in a lengthy address.

Mark 13:41 - *And He sat down opposite the treasury, and began observing how the multitude was putting money into the treasury.*

Luke 21:1 - *And He looked up and saw the rich putting their gifts into the treasury.*

Jesus had just endured two challenges to His person and work from the Pharisees and Sadducees, along with the Herodians, when He lashed out at the Pharisees with their legalistic religion. This speech included His denouncement of how they were devouring widows' homes. They were guilty of swallowing up inheritances so that they could be richer, leaving many widows destitute. With the significance of this day and Jesus' already strenuous encounters with His enemies, He sat down opposite the treasury, looked up, and observed how the people were casting their gifts into the collection boxes.

"...and He looked up and saw..."

A.T. Robertson in his book, *Word Pictures in the New Testament,* says "Mark draws the immortal picture of the weary Christ sitting down by the treasury." Christ was seeking a break from the constant onslaught and withdrew to the court of the women where the treasury was located. The multitudes shielded Him from further attack, and He pulled His disciples close and taught them an important lesson. From Jesus' sitting position, He was able to lean His head back against one of the colonnades and watch the people across the courtyard put money into the containers.

"...into the treasury."

The treasury was really thirteen trumpet-shaped containers laid out around the court of the women to receive the faithful's tithes and offerings. The receptacles were all identical with a wide bowl-shaped bottom and an opening that flared out to resemble a trumpet. Each container was marked for the arena in which its money would be spent. Nine of the receptacles were for the required giving of the Jews, and four were for the offerings that those who wanted to express devotion to God.

The text does not tell us that Jesus was watching the four trumpets reserved for free-will offerings, but the two subjects of the narrative (the rich and the widow) leave the impression that these were free-will offerings that Jesus was observing. The rich people were said to have given much out of their abundance, which would have been way beyond what they were required to tithe (ten percent). The widow gave all she had to live on, which was also more than what she was required to give.

"...He looked up and saw the rich putting their gifts into the treasury."
By far the majority of the people who were putting money into the free-will offering trumpets were those who had an abundance of goods. They had paid the tithe and still had furnished their lives with all they would reasonably need. They sought to return back to God some of His blessings to them. They gave much. Jesus had earlier condemned the fact that those who gave much would announce that they had given and often sound a horn or at least let their coins make a loud sound as they dropped to the bottom so that everyone could see and know that they were giving.

"...and many rich people were putting in large sums..."
In some way the rich were letting people know how much they were giving. Jesus, who sat across the courtyard, could tell that some were giving a lot and others were giving little.

The number of rich Jews giving offerings at the treasury would be increased because of the influx of pilgrims at the Passover Feast. This was the festival that every Jew would

The Widow's Mites

come to and would have stored up his tithes and offerings to bring them. As the pilgrims began arriving before the Passover, they would make their way to the temple and the court of the women, where they could deposit their stores in honor of the God who made them wealthy.

"and began observing how the multitude were putting money..."
Jesus began viewing this seemingly endless line of rich Jews who sought to make their mark on the rulers of the temple and even God. Jesus viewed the pompous pride of some, the humility of others, and the grudging nature of others. He was far more interested in the attitude of the giver than the amount of the gift. What is interesting is that He did not condemn those who gave much; He just pointed out that it is not the size of the gift that is the most crucial in determining its worth.

It is amazing that we can betray our heart attitude in as simple a manner as HOW we give our money to God. God understands where He ranks in your heart. One does not impress God by the size of the gift but the percentage of your heart that the gift represents. When one gives money, it is a tangible reflector of what percentage of your heart God has firmly in control.

"And He saw a certain poor widow putting in two small copper coins."
Having watched this endless parade of finely dressed men and women depositing huge surpluses of money into the treasury, Jesus' eye caught an obviously poor widow making her way

to the offering boxes. Her tattered clothes belied the fact that she had very little to live on. She should have been excused from the required offerings. What was she doing making her way to the free-will offerings? Her heart glowed with warmth for God. Her hands lovingly caressed her complete bank account -- two lepta. She dropped them so lovingly and freely. As she turned to go, no one stopped her for her contribution was minor. But the Spirit of the Living God moved the heart of Jesus to bring to light the incredible weight of her gift.

What we learn later is that Jesus was impressed by their attitude toward the money they gave to God. Did it reflect abandonment to God and His ways, or did it simply suggest that one does not know what to do with all of his money?

"...poor widow..."

Jesus referred to the widow using two different terms for poor. The first time He referred to the widow, He used the term *penichran*, which means *someone who has a minimal living, one who earns a paltry living*. This suggests that Jesus recognized that this woman had a job or income of some sort and that this income barely gave her enough to live on. The second word translated as poor in the NASB is the word *ptochi*, which means *someone who is destitute, who lives off gifts and the generosity of others*. Jesus used the word for a minimal living as the woman put the coins into the offering. It is possible that she was dressed in such a way as to tell clearly what meager job she had. Then Jesus used the word for destitute people after she gave her offering, which suggests that Jesus realized that this widow was now absolutely destitute, having given everything she had to God as an act of devotion.

In order to give a more lifelike picture to this widow from whom at present we have only a snapshot, let us take the clues given in Scripture to understand her situation. She was dressed in the garb of a poor person who had a menial job and barely enough to live on. She was obviously a widow -- a woman without a husband -- with no family to help her. This woman's job was servile at best and kept her poor. These types of jobs in Palestine were day labor jobs usually and at best paid weekly. Her income per day was probably the two lepta she put in the offering. Having given her day's wages to God as an act of consecration, she would have to wait until the next day or Friday to receive her next money which would not be enough. She literally chose to fast for one to two days so she could honor God. Freely in her heart she concocted this plan whereby she could love, honor, and bless God who sustained her in the midst of her loneliness and barren lifestyle. When was the last time you sacrificed in order to say to God, "I love you, God," in order to do what little you could to further the work of God?

"...two small copper coins, which amount to a cent."
The two coins the widow put in were lepta. Lepta were one of the coins that the Jews began minting under the Maccabean rule. It was a tiny bronze or copper coin that was extremely thin. The metal was the most inferior metal used in the minting of coins, and lepta were the smallest valued coin used in that day. The coins were like our pennies in that they were the bottom-rung on the coinage scale. The lepta had more spending power than our penny.

A lepton was half a quadrant. A quadrant was one-fourth an assarion. An assarion was one-sixteenth a denarius. A denarius was roughly equivalent to a common laborer's wages for one day. This means that if a common laborer makes $4 an hour, a lepton would be equivalent to roughly 25 cents. Someone who makes $4 an hour is considered poor, so let's pick a figure of $10 per hour, which could be considered the common laborer's wages or roughly $20,800 per year. This would make a lepton worth roughly 63 cents. The widow had two of these or $1.26.

The widow had only $1.26 to live on for who knows how long. And yet she was willing to put that money into the collection for God's work. What is interesting is that she certainly would not be putting her paltry sums into the collection to further the work of God. Instead, she seems to have deposited them in the collection to honor God, to speak of her love and devotion to God. It was her desire that God be lifted up even if it cost her food for the rest of the day or the rest of the week.

"...And calling His disciples to Him, He said to them..."
Jesus obviously wanted to make a point in the midst of this relaxation period. The disciples were probably resting and somewhat scattered around the colonnades of the treasury as Jesus watched intently on the proceedings around the collection areas. He called them over and they moved in to hear what He was going to say. One can almost hear Peter say, "Come on, Andrew. Our rest is over. Jesus wants us."

The Widow's Mites

"He said to them, 'Truly, I say to you, this poor widow put in more than all the contributions to the treasury.'"
Jesus' statement suggests that the widow was very close to Jesus by the time He got the disciples collected. It is even possible that He stopped her and she was standing in their midst. It was like Jesus to pull someone into the inner circle of the disciples and use them to teach a particular principle. The disciples, seeing the dress and destitution of the widow, could only have wondered at Jesus' comparison. What could He possibly mean by saying that she had thrown in more than all the others?

Jesus' style was to allow statements like this to sink in and to bubble up within a person until they understood what He meant. It is possible that the disciples did not see her casting her offering into the trumpet and that they thought maybe she was rich, but she didn't look rich. Maybe they thought Jesus was going to teach them how to dress and live in a humble fashion?

In order to capture the nature of the disciples' relationship with Jesus, we must understand that they constantly did not know what direction His statements would play out. Just when they thought they had Him figured out, He would apply a certain truth in a totally unique way. They sensed He was about to do it again, so they kept silent waiting for Jesus to explain why this widow had cast in more than all the rich.

"For they all put in out of their surplus…"
The rich that had contributed to the temple treasury were throwing in great sums. Some were announcing how much they gave. Others were trying to have as many people notice

them as possible. Some were just putting in huge amounts. But the common denominator for all those who gave was that what they gave was from their surplus. In other words, they had paid all the bills, they had tithed, they had bought what they wanted to buy, and they still had money left over. It was out of that surplus from which their offerings came.

"...but she out of her poverty put in all she owned, all she had to live on."
Jesus did not denigrate the rich person's offering because it was large. In fact, it was not the size that mattered at all. What matters in these types of equations is the pile of money it came from. There are two piles Jesus spoke of:

1. The perisseuonts (surplus) pile, where leftover money is stored.

2. The bion pile, which is the term Jesus used to describe whatever it takes to live on.

If someone offers $26,000 out of the surplus pile, it is not equivalent to $1.26 out of the necessity pile. In fact, anything coming out of the bion pile is worth more than the whole surplus pile.

If someone is going to give out of the bion pile, he or she must decide what to do without in order to give this money. The live-on pile is defined in Scripture as that which it takes to feed, clothe, and shelter us plus tithe and taxes. These five elements make up the bion pile and require that if you are going to give out of this pile, you must decide which of the three (food, clothing, or shelter) you are going to forgo so that you can give to God because you love Him. Now any amount in this pile is more than the whole of the surplus pile.

Delighting in Jesus

Giving offerings because of your desire to honor and thank God is a part of living a spiritual life. Many times in our day and age pastors and biblical teachers shrink back from talking about what Jesus says about giving and money. But Jesus was struck by what this poor widow did to give thanks and praise to God. This was an act of righteousness and Jesus noticed. It gets our attention what she did, but it also gets our attention that Jesus noticed this small act of righteousness. God is like that—He notices when we do the smallest things for the right reasons.

When was the last time you gave an offering to God over and above the tithe to just say to God, "I love you"? Look at your wallet or purse right now and see if you can set aside some of your spending money for an offering to God.

Conclusion

Jesus is delightful. Every story about Him is full of joy. I hope you have enjoyed this brief look at some of the episodes in Jesus' life and that it allowed you to take delight in Him in new ways around new truths. My desire is that it will whet your appetite for exploring other aspects and vignettes from the life of the Savior of the World. While many people say they know of Jesus and even believe in Him, there are few who have really become familiar with what He really said, did, and taught. He was different and revolutionary. He seeks to revolutionize your life. While any exploration of the Life of Jesus Christ is incomplete, the greatest completion would be your personal exploration and involvement in a relationship with Jesus Christ, the Savior and Lord of the World.

Let's remind ourselves of the journey that we have been on. We explored the following aspects of Jesus' life so we could embrace Him more fully and find His joy to be our joy.

The Baptism of Jesus
He was willing to submit to seemingly insignificant regulations and ceremonies to allow more people to connect with Him.

The Temptation of Jesus
He resisted the Devil's temptations through quoting the Word of God that was whispered to Him.

Jesus Visits His Hometown
A whole town was blocked from connecting with Jesus the miracle worker and the Messiah because they couldn't get over their memories and preconceived notions about Him.

The Feeding of the Five Thousand
God allowed Jesus to multiply bread to cause people to see His Son as the Messiah and all they saw was the bread.

Jesus Walks on the Water
Jesus challenged the faith of the disciples with a test after they had just seen Him multiply the fish and the loaves. Only Peter even attempted the test.

The Parable of the Sower
We are in charge of the condition of our soul. It is much like soil that the farmer prepares for his crops. God wants to plant His word in our soul, but it must be good soil or it won't amount to much.

Jesus' Discussion of Tragedy
Jesus slaps us across the face with the truth that we are all sinners and deserve death every day. We are to be grateful for each day and run to God for His mercy.

Jesus' Instruction on Prayer—Part 1

Jesus gave us five topics to talk to God about on a regular basis so that our basic spiritual connection is maintained. Most people only occasionally use one of the topics to converse with God.

Jesus' Instruction on Prayer—Part 2

Jesus talks with us about prayer and that the problem for a lack of answers is on our end rather than His end. We should shamelessly ask, seek, and knock. We can be confident that God the Father will not give us bad things. Talk to God more and ask for more.

The Widow's Mites

On Jesus' last full day of ministry before He was crucified, He pointed out a woman who gave a magnificent offering of all she had. Giving is an act of righteousness that has been under-developed in our spiritual lives.

If you do not know Jesus Christ as your personal Lord and Savior, I would invite you to pray this simple prayer:

Dear Lord Jesus,

I realize that I am a sinner and have no hope of heaven on my own. I want to take your sacrifice on the cross for the payment of my sins and follow you with my life. Please come into my life and make me the kind of person you want me to be. Thank you for living a perfect life and giving up your life for me. I do want you to come and run my life.

In the Name of the Lord Jesus Christ,
Amen.

For those of you who are more seasoned Christians, I would suggest you pray a prayer of delight in Jesus:

Dear Lord Jesus,

I thank you for taking my sins upon yourself so that I could have a relationship with you. I am delighted in you. I want to delight in you more and more. Thank you for teaching and training the disciples and allowing us to know the details of your training. I realize that there is so much more to who you are, what you did, and what you taught. Please draw me deeper into your person and let me be enraptured by you.

In the Name of the Lord Jesus Christ,
Amen.

Bibliography

Chapter 3
[1] Edershien, Alfred, *The Life and Times of Jesus the Messiah,* (Peabody: Hendrickson Pub; Updated edition July 1, 1993)

Chapter 4
[1] Edershien, Alfred, *The Life and Times of Jesus the Messiah,* (Peabody: Hendrickson Pub; Updated edition July 1, 1993)

[2] Edershien, Alfred, *The Life and Times of Jesus the Messiah,* (Peabody: Hendrickson Pub; Updated edition July 1, 1993)

[3] Edershien, Alfred, *The Life and Times of Jesus the Messiah,* (Peabody: Hendrickson Pub; Updated edition July 1, 1993)

Chapter 5
[1] Edershien, Alfred, *The Life and Times of Jesus the Messiah,* (Peabody: Hendrickson Pub; Updated edition July 1, 1993)

[2] Hendricksen, William, *Expostition of the Gospel of Luke,* (Ada: Baker Academic; 11th printing, September 2004 edition)

—**Chapter 7**
[1] Edershien, Alfred, *The Life and Times of Jesus the Messiah,* (Peabody: Hendrickson Pub; Updated edition July 1, 1993)

[2] Hendricksen, William, *Expostition of the Gospel of Luke,* (Ada: Baker Academic; 11th printing, September 2004 edition)

Chapter 8
[1]Wuest, Kenneth S., *Word Studies from the Greek New Testament*, (Grand Rapids: William B. Eerdmans Publishing Company; 2nd edition June 1, 1980)

Chapter 9
[1]Robertson, A.T. , *Word Pictures in the New Testament*, (Nashville: Broadman & Holman Bible Publishers; August 1, 2000)

About the Author

Gil Stieglitz is an internationally recognized author, speaker, catalyst, counselor, professor, and leadership consultant. He is currently Campus Pastor of Hillside Christian Church (Roseville, California), a Multi-site church in Texas and California. He has taught at several Christian universities and seminaries (BIOLA University, William Jessup University, Western Seminary). He is on the faculty of Principles to Live By, an organization committed to teaching God's principles in a life-giving way.

Other Resources by Gil Stieglitz

Becoming Courageous

Breakfast with Solomon Volume 1

Breakfast with Solomon Volume 2

Breaking Satanic Bondage

Deep Happiness: The Eight Secrets

Delighting in God

Developing a Christian Worldview

God's Radical Plan for Husbands

God's Radical Plan for Wives

Going Deep In Prayer: 40 Days of In-Depth Prayer

Leading a Thriving Ministry

Marital Intelligence

Mission Possible: Winning the Battle Over Temptation

Secrets of God's Armor

Spiritual Disciplines of a C.H.R.I.S.T.I.A.N

They Laughed When I Wrote Another Book About Prayer, Then They Read It

Touching the Face of God: 40 Days of Adoring God

Why There Has to Be a Hell

The Weapons of Righteousness Study Guide Series

The Spiritual Disciplines

The 10 Foundational Doctrines of Christianity

Basic Spiritual Warfare: The Three Enemies and The Four Weapons

Closing Spiritual Doorways

Podcasts

Becoming a Godly Parent

Biblical Meditation: The Keys of Transformation

Deep Happiness: The 8 Secrets

Everyday Spiritual Warfare Series

Intensive Spiritual Warfare Series

God's Guide to Handling Money

Spiritual War Surrounding Money

The Four Keys to a Great Family

The Ten Commandments

Thrive Conference

Marital Intelligence: There are Only Five Problems in Marriage

Raising Your Leadership Level: Double Your Impact

Spiritual Warfare: Using the Weapons of God to Win Spiritual Battles

Weapons of Righteousness Series

If you would be interested in having Gil Stieglitz speak to your group, you can contact Him through the website www.ptlb.com

www.ingramcontent.com/pod-product-compliance
Lightning Source LLC
Chambersburg PA
CBHW032107090426
42743CB00007B/270